Happy Children, Healthy Emotions: Help Your Child Name Feelings, Regulate Emotions, And Thrive

Mente Maestra

Table of contents

Introduction — Raising Kids Who Feel Deeply and Cope Well

It's the end of a long day. Shoes are kicked off, backpacks spill papers onto the floor, and someone is already crying because the blue cup is missing. You take a breath. You try to sound calm. "It's okay," you say, even though your own shoulders are tight. The tears get louder. A sibling rolls their eyes. Dinner is cooling on the counter. In moments like this, many parents wonder whether they're doing something wrong, or whether their child is simply "too sensitive." This book begins right here, in the ordinary chaos of family life, with a promise that feeling deeply is not a flaw to fix. It is a human capacity to guide.

There's a simple phrase you may have heard before: "Name it to tame it." It sounds catchy, maybe even simplistic, but it points to something powerful. When children can put words to what's happening inside them, their nervous system often settles enough for thinking to return. A feeling with a name is less overwhelming than a feeling that arrives like a storm with no map. When a child says, "I'm mad because you said no," or "I feel worried about school," something shifts. Their body gets a signal that the experience is understandable and shareable. This is not about stopping feelings. It's about making them workable.

Naming feelings doesn't magically erase tears or tantrums. What it does is create a bridge between emotion and action. A toddler who can say, "Frustrated," with your help, is learning that big sensations have edges and meaning. A school-age child who can say, "I'm embarrassed," is more likely to ask for help than to shut down or lash out. Even older children and adults benefit from this. When you quietly name your own state out loud, "I'm feeling overwhelmed and I need a minute," you're modeling the same skill. This book will return to that simple idea again and again, not as a trick, but as a foundation.

Many of us were raised with the idea that a "happy" child is a cheerful one. We learned to praise smiles and worry about tears. But happiness, in the deeper sense, does not mean always upbeat or easygoing. It means emotionally safe, flexible, and connected. A child who feels safe knows their inner world is welcome, even when it's messy. A child who is flexible can move through disappointment without breaking. A child who feels connected trusts that relationships can stretch and repair after hard moments. Cheerfulness comes and goes. Emotional safety lasts longer.

You may notice this difference in real life. A child who is always smiling but terrified of disappointing adults is not necessarily thriving. A child who argues, cries, and then settles with support may actually be developing strong coping skills. The goal here is not to raise children who never melt down, but children who can move through intense feelings and return to connection. That return matters. It's where learning happens.

This book rests on three pillars that support that kind of growth. The first is emotional vocabulary. Children need words for their inner experience the same way they need words for colors and shapes. Without language, feelings stay stuck in the body. With language, they become shareable and less frightening. Throughout the chapters, you'll find everyday ways to build this vocabulary without quizzes or lectures, using moments that are already happening.

The second pillar is regulation skills. Regulation is the ability to notice feelings and help the body settle. Young children borrow this skill from adults. Over time, they begin to internalize it. Regulation is not about suppressing emotion or demanding calm. It's about offering enough support so the nervous system can come back to balance. This might look like breathing together, movement, sensory comfort, or quiet presence. You'll learn how to choose what fits your child and the moment, without forcing one "right" technique.

The third pillar is relationship repair. No family gets it right all the time. Voices rise. Doors slam. Words land harder than intended. What matters most is not avoiding rupture, but repairing it. Repair teaches children that conflict doesn't end connection. It teaches responsibility without shame and trust without perfection. When you circle back after a hard moment and say, "That was tough. Let's talk about it," you're building resilience in a way no lecture ever could.

Some changes will happen quickly when you start practicing these ideas. You may notice that your child uses a feeling word you've modeled, or that a meltdown shortens by a few minutes. You might catch yourself pausing instead of reacting, or hear your child ask for a hug instead of throwing something. These are real shifts. Other changes take time. A child who has spent years without support for big feelings may need months of steady practice before new patterns stick. Progress is not linear. There will be easier weeks and harder ones, especially during transitions, illness, or stress.

So how do you measure real progress at home? Not by counting tantrums or aiming for constant peace. Instead, look for subtle markers. Notice how long it takes to reconnect after a hard moment. Notice whether your child recovers more quickly, or whether they're willing to talk about what happened later. Notice whether you feel a little less helpless when emotions run high. These are signs that skills are growing, even when life still feels loud.

As you begin, it can help to set a gentle intention rather than a rigid goal. For example, you might decide to listen for one feeling a day and name it out loud. Or you might practice repairing one small rupture each evening. Keep your expectations human. You are learning alongside your child.

To use this book, pick one chapter per week. Read it slowly, maybe in the quiet of early morning or after bedtime. Then practice for ten minutes a day. Ten minutes is long enough to matter and short enough to be realistic. You don't need special tools or a perfectly calm household. You need willingness and repetition.

Here is a simple ten-minute daily practice you can start today. Choose a predictable moment, like bedtime or after school. Sit with your child, or if they're older, take a short walk together. Begin by sharing one feeling from your own day, keeping it age-appropriate. You might say, "Today I felt frustrated when traffic was slow, and I took a few breaths to help my body settle." Then invite your child to share one feeling. If they struggle, offer options. "Did today feel more fun, boring, or hard?" When a feeling comes up, reflect it back. "That sounds disappointing." Pause for a few breaths together, or place a hand on your chest and invite your child to do the same. End by naming one thing that helped, even if it was small. "Talking together helped me." This entire exchange can take ten minutes or less. Over time, it builds a rhythm of awareness, regulation, and connection.

You'll find scripts throughout this book that you can adapt to your own voice. For example, in the heat of a moment, you might say, "I see how big this feels. I'm here." Or after things calm down, "Earlier was hard. What do you think was going on for you?" These are not magic words. They are invitations. If they don't land perfectly, that's okay. The tone matters more than the phrasing.

Each section also includes a short practice you can try right away. Think of these as experiments, not tests. If something doesn't fit your child or your family, set it aside and try another approach.

Children vary widely in temperament, sensory needs, and developmental stage. A strategy that soothes a toddler may irritate a ten-year-old. Curiosity will serve you better than rigidity.

A gentle note about support. This book is meant to guide everyday parenting, not to replace professional care. If your child's emotions feel unmanageable, if there are concerns about safety, self-harm, aggression, or prolonged distress, or if your own stress feels overwhelming, reaching out to a qualified professional is a wise and caring step. Support is a resource, not a failure.

As you read on, remember that raising kids who feel deeply and cope well is not about controlling emotions. It's about building capacity, together. You are not expected to be endlessly patient or perfectly regulated. You are expected to be real, responsive, and willing to repair. That is more than enough to begin.

Chapter 1 Feelings Have a Job: The New Map of Children's Emotions

It's easy to think a child is "overreacting" when the reaction looks bigger than the situation. A cracker breaks. A game ends. A sock feels wrong. The tears come fast and loud. From the outside, it can feel confusing or even manipulative. From the inside of a child's body, it's usually something else entirely. Kids aren't built with adult-sized brakes for self-control yet, and they're still learning how to steer with language. When the brakes are weak and the steering wheel is small, emotions come out sideways.

Imagine a four-year-old whose tower collapses. To an adult, it's just blocks. To the child, it's effort, hope, and identity falling over at once. Their brain hasn't finished wiring the parts that slow impulses or explain feelings with words. The feeling hits the body first. Shoulders tense. Breath gets shallow. The urge to yell or throw arrives before the thought, "I'm disappointed." That's not defiance. It's development in motion.

Or picture a ten-year-old who snaps at a sibling after school. The words are sharp. The tone is rude. It might look like a choice to be mean. But this child has spent six hours holding it together, navigating noise, rules, and social pressure. By the time they walk through the door, the tank is empty. The feeling that spills out might be irritation, but the job of that feeling is to say, "I'm overloaded and I need relief." When we read behavior as a message instead of a verdict, our response changes.

This chapter offers a new map for understanding children's emotions. Instead of asking, "How do I stop this behavior?" we begin with, "What is this feeling trying to do?" Feelings have jobs. They signal needs, protect us from danger, and push us toward connection or rest. When we miss the message, the feeling usually gets louder. When we hear it, the intensity often softens.

This doesn't mean all behavior is acceptable. It means we separate the feeling from the action. A child can be furious and still not allowed to hit. A child can be heartbroken and still expected to use kind words. Limits matter. They just land better when the child feels understood first.

A short script that de-escalates without shaming might sound like this: "I see how big this feels. I won't let you hit, and I'm here to help you calm." It's brief, clear, and respectful. It names the feeling's weight while holding the boundary steady.

Here's a simple practice you can try this week. Once a day, pick a moment when emotions are mild, not explosive. It might be after a small disappointment or during play. Gently narrate what you see without judgment. "Your face scrunched up when the piece didn't fit. That looked frustrating." Then pause. Let your child respond or not. The practice isn't to fix the feeling, but to notice it together. Over time, this builds a shared language that makes bigger moments easier.

As you work with this new map, remember that learning happens in layers. Some days you'll catch the feeling early. Other days you'll realize it afterward. Both count. If emotions feel extreme, persistent, or tied to safety concerns, reaching out to a qualified professional can provide additional support. Asking for help is part of caring for your child and yourself.

1.1 Emotions as Messages, Not Misbehavior

When children act in ways we don't like, it's tempting to label the behavior and move on. "Rude." "Lazy." "Attention-seeking."

Labels feel efficient, but they stop curiosity. Emotions, on the other hand, invite decoding. Most so-called "bad behavior" is linked to unmet needs like fatigue, hunger, overwhelm, or disconnection. The behavior is the smoke, not the fire.

Think of a two-year-old who throws food at the end of dinner. It's easy to see disrespect. It's more accurate to see exhaustion or overstimulation. The throwing is the child's clumsy way of saying, "I'm done." Or consider an eight-year-old who refuses homework with a dramatic slump and a sigh. Beneath the refusal might be discouragement or fear of getting something wrong. When we respond only to the surface, we miss the chance to teach coping.

Understanding the difference between emotion and behavior changes discipline. Emotion is internal. It's what's happening inside the body and mind. Behavior is external. It's what we can see and hear. We don't discipline emotions. We guide behavior. When we punish a feeling, children learn to hide it or act it out later. When we guide behavior while respecting emotion, children learn skills.

This is where the emotion cycle helps. A trigger happens. The body reacts with signals like a racing heart or tight stomach. A feeling forms, such as anger or sadness. An impulse follows, maybe to yell or run. An action happens. Then there's a consequence, internal or external. If we intervene at the action alone, we miss several earlier steps. If we help children notice body signals and name feelings, we can slow the cycle before it explodes.

Here's a real-life example with a preschooler. A five-year-old is told it's time to leave the playground. The trigger is the transition. The body signal is tension and faster movement. The feeling is disappointment. The impulse is to run away. The action is bolting toward the slide. The consequence is a power struggle. A parent who understands the cycle might kneel and say, "Leaving is hard. Your body wants more play." Then they set the limit. "It's time to go, and I'll help you walk." The child may still cry, but the message has been heard.

Now an older example. A twelve-year-old slams a door after being asked to turn off a game. The trigger is interruption. The body signal is adrenaline. The feeling might be frustration mixed with embarrassment. The impulse is to escape. The action is the door slam. The consequence is tension. Later, when things are calmer, a parent can circle back. "Earlier, the door slam told me you were really upset. Next time, let's find words that keep the door safe." This separates the feeling from the behavior and invites learning.

A short parent script that de-escalates without shaming could be: "I won't let you talk that way, and I want to understand what you're feeling." It holds the line and opens a door.

Here's a brief practice for this section. Choose one recurring behavior that frustrates you. For a few days, don't try to fix it immediately. Instead, quietly track the pattern in your mind. When does it happen? What came right before? Is your child tired, hungry, rushed, or disconnected? Then try reflecting the likely feeling once. "I wonder if you're overwhelmed." Say it as a guess, not a fact. Notice what changes. Sometimes the behavior softens. Sometimes it doesn't. Either way, you're building insight.

As you practice decoding, keep compassion for yourself. Old habits of labeling are hard to unlearn, especially when you're stressed. Progress might look like catching yourself mid-sentence and choosing a different response. That counts. And again, if behaviors feel intense, unsafe, or beyond what you can manage at home, seeking professional guidance is a supportive step, not a defeat.

In the next section, we'll look at what happens in children's brains under stress, and why staying calm yourself is one of the most powerful tools you have.

1.2 The Three Brain Systems Kids Use Under Stress

When a child melts down, it can feel personal. You asked calmly. You explained why. You even gave a warning. And still, the reaction was explosive. This is where understanding what happens in the brain under stress changes everything. Kids don't "overreact" because they want to make life harder. They overreact because the parts of the brain that help them pause, explain, and choose are still under construction.

Under stress, children rely heavily on what's often called the survival brain. This system's job is simple: keep the body safe. When it senses threat, whether that threat is real danger or just a sudden change, it prepares the body to fight, flee, or freeze. Heart rate increases. Muscles tense. Thinking narrows. In this state, logic doesn't land. Long explanations sound like noise. Asking a child to "use your words" when the survival brain is in charge is like asking someone to solve a puzzle while running from a loud alarm.

You've likely seen this with a young child who collapses on the floor screaming when it's time to leave a birthday party. Or with an older child who shuts down completely after a critical comment. Their reaction isn't a choice in that moment. It's a reflex. The brain has decided something is too much, and it's pulling the emergency brake.

Many parents find it helpful to think in terms of an "upstairs" and "downstairs" brain. The upstairs brain handles reasoning, planning, and empathy. The downstairs brain handles survival and big emotions. When kids are calm, both floors are connected. When stress hits, the downstairs brain takes over, and the upstairs brain goes temporarily offline. This explains why a child who knows the rules can't follow them during a meltdown, and why lectures during these moments rarely work.

A real-life example can make this clearer. Picture a seven-year-old who explodes when a sibling touches their Lego build. In a calm moment, this child understands sharing and can explain their feelings. In the heat of the moment, the downstairs brain is driving. The touching feels like a threat to something important. The reaction is fast and physical. Telling them, "You know better," assumes the upstairs brain is available. It isn't.

This is where co-regulation comes in. Co-regulation is the process by which an adult's calm helps a child's nervous system settle. It's not about being perfectly serene. It's about being steadier than your child in that moment. Your tone, posture, and pacing matter more than your words. When you lower your voice, slow your movements, and stay present, you're lending your child your regulation until they can find their own.

Over time, repeated experiences of being calmed by another person help children build internal skills. A toddler who is rocked and soothed eventually learns to take a breath. A school-age child who hears, "I'm here, we'll figure this out," begins to say that to themselves. Self-regulation grows out of co-regulation. It doesn't replace it overnight.

A simple parent script during a meltdown might be, "I see you're really upset. I'm here, and we'll wait until your body feels calmer." This doesn't fix everything, but it sends a clear signal of safety.

There are common mistakes that can get in the way here. One is trying to reason too early, explaining consequences or lessons while the child is still flooded. Another is matching the child's intensity with your own raised voice or sharp movements, which can escalate the survival response. A third is withdrawing completely, assuming the child needs to "cool off" alone when what they actually need is a steady presence. None of these make you a bad parent. They're understandable reactions under stress. Awareness simply gives you more options.

Here's a tiny practice you can try today. The next time you notice your child getting dysregulated, check your own body first. Soften your shoulders. Take one slow breath. Lower your voice by a notch. Say less than you think you need to. This might take less than thirty seconds, but it can change the tone of the entire interaction.

After a hard moment, repair matters. Imagine you raised your voice when your child was melting down. Later, when things are calm, you might say, "Earlier, I got loud when you were upset. I wish I had slowed down. Next time, I'll try to help us both calm." This models accountability without shame and shows that relationships can recover.

If your child's reactions seem extreme, frequent, or tied to safety concerns, additional support from a qualified professional can be helpful. Understanding the brain is empowering, but you don't have to do this alone.

1.3 Building an Emotion-Friendly Home Culture

Individual moments matter, but culture shapes what those moments mean. An emotion-friendly home culture is not one where everyone is calm all the time. It's one where feelings are allowed, talked about, and guided. It's a place where emotions don't earn ridicule or threats, and where behavior is still held to clear limits.

Culture is built from small, repeated signals. When feelings are mocked, even jokingly, children learn to hide them. When kids are labeled as "dramatic" or "too sensitive," they internalize those stories. When threats are used to control behavior, fear replaces trust. Shifting this doesn't require perfection. It requires intention.

In an emotion-friendly home, feelings are normalized without giving them the final say. A child can be angry and still expected to keep hands to themselves. A child can be sad and still go to school. The message is, "Your feelings make sense, and we still have rules." This balance is where emotional safety grows.

Consider a bedtime scene with a three-year-old who suddenly protests going to bed. Tears appear. The body stiffens. Instead of saying, "Stop crying, it's bedtime," a parent might say, "You wish the day could keep going. Bedtime is hard." Then the limit follows. "It's still time to sleep, and I'll stay with you for a minute." The feeling is honored. The boundary holds.

With an older child, imagine a nine-year-old who is furious about a lost game. They stomp and shout. An emotion-friendly response might sound like, "Losing really hurts. I won't let you yell at people." Then comes guidance. "Let's find a way to let the anger out safely." The child learns that emotions are not dangerous, but actions matter.

A daily emotional check-in can support this culture without turning your home into a therapy session. The key is keeping it light and predictable. It might happen at dinner, in the car, or before bed. Each person shares one feeling from the day and one thing that helped or made it easier. For young children, you can offer choices. "Did today feel more fun or more hard?" For older kids, you might simply model by sharing first. "Today I felt nervous before a meeting, and taking a walk helped." Over time, this ritual builds emotional literacy and connection.

A short script that keeps things safe could be, "All feelings are okay here. Not all actions are." Simple, clear, and repeatable.

There are common pitfalls to watch for. One is turning check-ins into interrogations, pushing for details when a child isn't ready. Another is rushing to fix or advise instead of listening. A third is inconsistency, allowing mocking or harsh words when you're tired, then correcting them later. Again, these are human slips, not failures. Noticing them is the first step to change.

Here's a small practice to try today. Choose one phrase you'll use consistently to normalize feelings. It might be, "That makes sense," or "I can see why you'd feel that way." Use it once, sincerely, when your child shares something emotional. Notice how it shifts the conversation, even slightly.

Repair after rupture is part of culture too. Imagine a morning where everyone is rushed and tempers flare. Doors slam. Words are sharp. Later that evening, you might gather your child and say, "This morning felt rough. I don't like how we spoke to each other. Let's reset." You can invite your child to share, but you don't require it. The act of naming and repairing teaches that hard moments don't define the relationship.

As you build this culture, remember that change is gradual. Some children test safety by expressing more once they feel heard. This can feel like things are getting worse before they get better. Stay steady. Track small signs of progress, like quicker recovery or more honest sharing.

And always hold space for extra help when needed. If emotions in your home feel overwhelming, if conflicts escalate toward harm, or if you're feeling burned out, reaching out to a professional can provide guidance tailored to your family. An emotion-friendly culture includes knowing when to ask for support.

In the weeks ahead, these foundations will help you move from reacting to guiding, from controlling behavior to teaching skills. Feelings will still be big. That's part of childhood. But with a supportive map and steady practice, they can become signals to understand rather than storms to fear.

Chapter 2 The Feelings Dictionary: Teaching Kids to Name What's Real

Many children say "I'm fine" not because they are fine, but because they don't yet have words for what's actually happening inside. "Fine" can mean conflicted, left out, overstimulated, disappointed, or a mix of three feelings at once. When language is limited, children default to the safest, shortest answer. This chapter is about giving kids a richer dictionary for their inner world, so "fine" slowly becomes more specific, more honest, and more useful.

Imagine a six-year-old coming home from school, tossing their backpack down, and shrugging when asked how their day was. "Fine." Later that evening, they explode over a small request. The explosion doesn't come out of nowhere. It's the backlog of unnamed experiences finally spilling out. Or think of a three-year-old who cries and clings after a playdate. They can't say, "I felt left out when they didn't let me choose the game," so their body does the talking instead.

Words don't make feelings bigger. They make them clearer. When a child can name what's real, the nervous system often settles enough to allow problem-solving and connection. This doesn't mean kids will suddenly give eloquent emotional speeches. It means they'll have more than one option besides silence or meltdown.

Teaching emotional language is not a one-time lesson. It's a slow, relational process that happens in the middle of real life. It happens when you name your own feelings out loud in simple ways. It happens when you reflect what you see without correcting or analyzing. It happens when words are offered, not demanded.

A short parent script that de-escalates without shaming might sound like this: "You're saying you're fine, and I wonder if there's more there. We can take our time." This leaves the door open without pressure.

Here's a small practice you can start this week. Pick one moment a day to name a feeling you see in your child, even if they don't respond. Keep it brief and neutral. "That looked frustrating," or "You seem disappointed." You're planting seeds. Some will sprout right away. Others will take weeks. Both count.

As you work on this chapter, remember that naming feelings is a skill, not a personality trait. Some children love words. Others need more time, play, or distance before language comes. Your job is to offer vocabulary, not to force fluency. If your child's emotional expression feels blocked by fear, intense distress, or safety concerns, extra support from a qualified professional can be helpful. Language grows best where safety exists.

2.1 From Basic to Precise: Expanding Emotional Vocabulary

Most children begin with a small set of core feelings. Mad. Sad. Glad. Scared. These are excellent starting points. They are broad enough to catch many experiences and simple enough to remember. The goal is not to rush past them, but to build outward slowly, adding nuance as children grow.

A four-year-old who says "mad" might mean frustrated, disappointed, jealous, or overwhelmed. An eight-year-old who says "sad" might actually feel embarrassed or left out. When we accept the basic word and gently offer a more precise one, we help children refine their understanding without invalidating their experience.

You might hear this in a real-life moment with a preschooler whose drawing ripped. They yell, "I'm mad!" Instead of correcting, you can join them where they are. "Yes, mad. It looks like frustrated mad because it didn't work the way you wanted." The child doesn't have to repeat the new word. Just hearing it expands their internal map.

With an older child, nuance becomes even more important. A ten-year-old who says, "I hate school," may be dealing with disappointment after a poor grade or worry about fitting in. You might respond, "I hear how strong that feels. Is it more disappointed, more worried, or something else?" This invites specificity without arguing about the content.

One helpful way to think about this process is as an emotion ladder. You start at the bottom with a vague or general feeling, then gently move upward toward something more precise. The ladder is not something you show or lecture about. It's something you use in conversation. A child says, "I'm upset." You reflect, "Upset can mean lots of things. Is it more mad or more sad?" If they choose mad, you might offer, "Is it annoyed mad or really angry mad?" Each step gives them more choice and control.

Teaching intensity is another important layer. Feelings come in degrees. Annoyed is different from angry. Angry is different from furious. Nervous is different from scared. Scared is different from terrified. When children learn this, they gain a sense of proportion. Not every uncomfortable feeling means disaster. Some are small and manageable. Others are big and need more support.

A vivid example comes from a seven-year-old who panics before a spelling test. They say, "I'm scared." A parent might respond, "Let's check the size of that scared. Is it nervous scared, or really scared?" The child thinks and says, "Just nervous." That single word shift can lower intensity and open space for coping.

For younger children, you can model intensity through play. When stacking blocks, you might exaggerate and say, "I'm a tiny bit annoyed," when a block wobbles, and "Now I'm very frustrated," when it falls. Play gives children a low-stakes way to hear and feel the differences.

A short parent script that supports this without shaming could be: "That feeling sounds strong. Let's find the right word for how big it is." It frames the task as collaborative, not corrective.

Here's a simple practice for this section. Choose one basic feeling your child uses often, like mad or sad. For a few days, listen for opportunities to add one new related word in context. Don't quiz. Just sprinkle it in. "That's a disappointed kind of sad." Notice if your child starts to echo it later, even weeks from now.

It's also important to name your own feelings with nuance. Saying, "I'm frustrated because I'm running late," teaches more than saying, "I'm mad." Children learn vocabulary by hearing it used honestly and calmly. This doesn't mean sharing adult worries. It means narrating everyday emotions in a way that models precision.

There are common mistakes to avoid as you expand emotional language. One is overcorrecting, insisting a child use the "right" word instead of accepting their attempt. Another is overwhelming them with too many options at once. A third is using emotional words only during conflict, which can make them feel heavy or punitive. Keep the tone light and the pace slow.

Repair still matters here too. Imagine a moment where you push too hard, asking again and again, "What are you feeling?" and your child shuts down. Later, you can say, "Earlier I kept asking about your feelings, and that felt like too much. I'm sorry. We can talk when you're ready." This teaches that emotional conversations are flexible and respectful.

As you build this feelings dictionary week by week, remember that the goal is usefulness, not sophistication. A child who can say "I'm frustrated" instead of throwing a toy has gained a powerful tool. A child who can say "I'm disappointed but I'll try again" is practicing resilience in real time. These shifts are subtle and cumulative.

And always hold space for the fact that some children need more support to access language, especially during stress. If naming feelings consistently feels impossible or distressing for your child, or if emotional expression is tied to significant struggles at home or school, reaching out for professional guidance can provide tailored strategies and reassurance.

In the next sections, you'll explore tools and playful approaches that make naming feelings easier, even for shy or reluctant kids. For now, stay with the basics. Offer words. Listen. Let "fine" slowly turn into something more real.

2.2 Tools That Make Naming Easy (Even for Shy Kids)

Some children love to talk. Others need an invitation that doesn't feel like a spotlight. Tools can help bridge that gap, not by pushing kids to perform, but by giving them something to point to, play with, or notice together. When tools are used gently, they take pressure off language and make naming feelings feel safer.

Feeling charts, mood wheels, and emotion cards are often marketed as solutions, but their power depends on how they're used. If a chart becomes a quiz or a requirement, many kids shut down. If it becomes a shared reference, it can open conversation. Imagine a chart on the fridge with simple faces and words. After school, instead of asking, "How are you feeling?" you might say, "I'm going to point to how I felt today. I was here for a while, then here." You model first. Your child watches without being put on the spot. Later, they may point on their own. Or they may not. Both are okay.

For a shy five-year-old, a parent once noticed that direct questions led to silence. They tried something different. During snack, they casually held up two emotion cards. "I'm choosing between calm and tired for me." The child leaned over and touched the tired card. No words were needed. The moment counted. Over time, the child began adding single words. The tool created a low-pressure on-ramp.

Mood wheels can be especially helpful for older children who feel embarrassed by "babyish" charts. A wheel that shows broad categories with smaller, more precise words around the edges allows kids to start vague and move inward. You might say, "I'm somewhere in the stressed area today." That's it. You don't ask them to explain. The wheel does some of the work for you.

Games can also make naming feelings easier. A simple "guess my feeling" game uses faces, body posture, and tone. You exaggerate a feeling with your body and voice, and your child guesses. You might slump your shoulders and sigh. "What do you think I'm feeling?" Or you might stomp dramatically. "This one's big." The point isn't accuracy. It's noticing cues. Younger children love the silliness. Older children often join in once they see it's playful, not performative.

Story-based labeling is another powerful tool because it creates distance. When feelings belong to a character, not the child, defensiveness drops. While reading a book or watching a show, you can pause and wonder out loud. "Her face changed when that happened. I wonder if she felt left out." You're not asking your child to disclose anything. You're modeling curiosity. Many children will spontaneously connect. "That happened to me once," they might say. Even if they don't, they're absorbing the language.

A vivid example comes from an eight-year-old who resisted talking about school. During a movie, a character was excluded from a game. The parent paused and said, "That looks disappointing." The child nodded and quietly added, "Yeah." Later that week, after a rough day, the same child said, "I think I felt like that character." The tool created a bridge.

A short parent script that keeps things light could be, "We don't have to talk about you. Let's see what the character might be feeling." This removes pressure while still practicing the skill.

There are common mistakes to avoid with tools. One is using them only during conflict, which can make them feel like discipline devices. Another is insisting on participation, turning pointing or guessing into a demand. A third is overloading with too many options, which can overwhelm instead of help. Tools work best when they're available, not mandatory.

Here's a tiny practice to try today. Choose one tool you already have, or even draw a simple face with two expressions. Place it somewhere visible. Use it once for yourself, briefly and honestly. Then let it be. Notice if your child engages later, even in a small way.

Repair applies here too. Imagine you pushed a chart in front of your child and said, "Just pick one," and they snapped, "Stop!" Later, you might say, "I tried to get you to choose a feeling earlier, and that felt pushy. I'm sorry. We can use it when you want." This restores safety and trust.

As always, remember that tools are supports, not solutions. Some children need more time, play, or distance to access language. If your child consistently avoids naming feelings and seems distressed, or if communication around emotions feels stuck, additional support from a qualified professional can help tailor approaches to your child's needs.

2.3 When Kids Say "I Don't Know"

Few phrases frustrate parents more than "I don't know." It can sound dismissive or defiant, especially when you're trying to connect. Often, though, "I don't know" is the most honest answer a child can give in that moment. It usually points to one of three things: fear of consequences, overwhelm, or low self-awareness.

Fear of consequences shows up when children worry that naming a feeling will get them in trouble or disappoint you. A child who learned that anger leads to lectures or punishment may protect themselves with "I don't know." Overwhelm happens when the feeling is too big or too mixed to sort out quickly. Low self-awareness is common in younger kids and in moments of stress. They genuinely don't have access to the information yet.

Understanding this changes how we respond. Instead of pushing harder, we soften. Instead of interrogating, we offer gentle structure. A question like, "Why are you upset?" can feel like a trap. A prompt like, "Is it more mad or more sad?" narrows the field and reduces pressure.

Imagine a ten-year-old who had a conflict with a friend and comes home withdrawn. When asked how they feel, they shrug. "I don't know." A parent might respond, "That's okay. Sometimes it's hard to tell. Is it closer to mad or closer to sad?" The child pauses and says, "Sad, I guess." That single word is a start.

For younger children, you can use even simpler prompts. "Does your body feel tight or heavy?" Or, "Does it feel like you want to cry or yell?" These questions anchor feelings in physical sensations, which are often easier to access.

Creating a safe exit is also important. Children need to know they're not trapped in a conversation. You might say, "You don't have to use words. You can show me with a color, a number, or a drawing." A child might grab a red crayon and scribble hard. That tells you something without forcing language.

A real-life example comes from a five-year-old who froze whenever asked about preschool. One evening, the parent set out paper and markers without comment. The child drew a small figure alone on one side of the page. The parent gently said, "That looks lonely." The child nodded. No more was needed that night. The drawing did the talking.

A short parent script that de-escalates without shaming could be, "You don't have to know right now. I'm here when it comes." This reassures without pushing.

Common mistakes in these moments include repeating the same question louder, assuming the child is being stubborn, or filling the silence with your own guesses presented as facts. Another is giving up entirely, interpreting "I don't know" as refusal rather than information. Balance matters.

Here's a tiny practice to try today. The next time your child says, "I don't know," respond with one validating sentence and then pause. For example, "That makes sense. Sometimes feelings take a minute." Count to ten silently before saying anything else. The pause itself can be an invitation.

Repair after a hard moment can deepen trust. Imagine you pressed for answers and your child shut down completely. Later, you might say, "Earlier I kept asking how you felt, and that felt overwhelming. I'm sorry. We can try again another time." This shows respect for your child's pace.

As you move through this chapter, keep the long view in mind. The goal is not immediate clarity, but growing capacity. Each time you respond to "I don't know" with patience instead of pressure, you teach that confusion is acceptable and connection is steady.

And remember, if "I don't know" is paired with significant distress, withdrawal, or safety concerns, it's wise to seek additional support. Professionals can help uncover what's beneath the freeze and offer strategies suited to your child's temperament and experiences.

In the coming chapters, you'll build on this language work by helping children regulate their bodies and repair relationships after big feelings. For now, stay gentle. Words will come when safety leads the way.

Chapter 3 The Body Is the First Clue: Teaching Kids to Read Sensations

Before children can say, "I'm anxious," their body usually speaks first. A belly tightens. Cheeks get hot. Legs won't stop moving. Hands clench. This is not a failure of language or attitude. It's biology doing its job. The body detects change and prepares to respond long before words arrive. When we help kids notice those early signals, we give them a head start on coping.

Think about a two-year-old who suddenly drops to the floor in the grocery store. To an adult, it looks abrupt and confusing. To the child's body, it's a flood of noise, lights, and waiting. The body says, "Too much," long before the mind can explain it. Or picture a nine-year-old who insists they're "fine" but can't sit still before a class presentation. Their legs bounce, their breathing is shallow, and their jaw is tight. The body is already telling the story.

This chapter builds on the language work you began in Chapter 2. Words matter, but they come second. Sensations come first. When children learn to read their bodies, they gain an early-warning system. They can notice what's building and respond sooner, with less intensity. This doesn't eliminate big feelings. It makes them more predictable and manageable.

Many adults were taught to ignore or override body signals. "You're not hungry." "You're fine." "Don't be so sensitive." When kids grow up disconnected from their bodies, emotions can feel sudden and overwhelming. Reconnecting doesn't mean becoming hyper-focused on every sensation. It means learning a simple, friendly awareness. What is my body telling me right now?

A short parent script that de-escalates without shaming might sound like this: "I see your legs moving fast. That's a clue your body is feeling something." It names the observation without judgment and invites curiosity instead of control.

Here's a gentle practice you can try this week. Once a day, during a calm moment, narrate one body sensation you notice in yourself. "My shoulders feel tight. I think I need a stretch." Keep it brief. You're modeling how to listen inward without alarm. Over time, children begin to mirror this awareness.

As always, if body reactions feel extreme, confusing, or connected to safety concerns, professional support can help clarify what's going on and offer additional strategies. Learning body awareness should feel supportive, not scary.

3.1 Body Signals 101 (Kid-Friendly Interoception)

Interoception is a big word for a simple idea: noticing what's happening inside the body. Kids don't need the word. They need the skill. When children can identify body cues linked to different emotions, they gain a powerful tool for self-understanding.

Stress often shows up as a tight belly, shallow breathing, or restless movement. Anger might feel like heat in the face, clenched fists, or a pounding chest. Sadness can feel heavy, slow, or achy, like a lump in the throat. Excitement might feel buzzy, wiggly, or fast. Shame is trickier. It often shows up as wanting to hide, a dropped gaze, or a flushed face. None of these sensations are good or bad. They're information.

A vivid example comes from a five-year-old who frequently hit during playdates. The behavior was the focus for a long time.

When a parent slowed down and began noticing body cues, they saw a pattern. Right before hitting, the child's shoulders lifted and their breathing sped up. During a calm moment, the parent said, "I noticed your shoulders go up like this before things get hard." They practiced shrugging and relaxing together. Over time, the child began to recognize the feeling earlier and ask for help instead of lashing out.

With older kids, the process looks different but the principle is the same. An eleven-year-old might complain of a stomachache every Sunday night. Instead of dismissing it or assuming avoidance, a parent can explore gently. "Let's check in with your body. Does it feel tight, twisty, or heavy?" The child might say, "Tight." That's a clue. It opens the door to naming worry or dread without forcing a confession.

Activities that ask, "Where do you feel it?" build this awareness in a concrete way. For younger children, you can turn it into a game. "When you're mad, where does your body feel it most?" They might point to their hands or stomp their feet. You accept the answer as information, not something to fix. For older children, you can ask during calm times, "When you get nervous, what's the first thing your body does?" These conversations are easier when emotions are low.

Spotting early-warning signs is one of the most useful outcomes of this work. Meltdowns rarely come out of nowhere. There's usually a build-up. A toddler may get louder and clumsier. A school-age child may get sarcastic or withdrawn. When you help children notice these signals, you help them intervene earlier. "My belly feels tight" can become a cue to take a break, get a snack, or ask for support.

A short parent script during these moments might be, "Your body looks like it's getting overwhelmed. Let's pause." It's simple and respectful.

There are common mistakes to avoid when teaching body awareness. One is turning it into constant monitoring, which can make kids anxious. Another is correcting a child's interpretation. If they say anger feels like "fire ants," you don't need to translate it into something more accurate. Their metaphor is valid. A third mistake is waiting until a meltdown to talk about body cues, when the learning window is small. Practice works best in calm moments.

Here's a tiny practice to try today. During a relaxed moment, invite your child to do a quick body scan with you. You might say, "Let's check in from head to toe. Anything feel tight or loose?" Keep it under a minute. End with something grounding, like a stretch or a sip of water. This builds awareness without intensity.

Repair is part of this learning too. Imagine you misread a body signal and said, "You're tired," when your child felt angry. They snapped back. Later, you can say, "Earlier I guessed wrong about what your body was feeling. Thanks for telling me. I'm still learning." This models flexibility and respect for their internal experience.

As you continue through this chapter, remember that body awareness develops gradually. Some children connect quickly. Others need repetition and play. Your steady curiosity matters more than accuracy. If a child struggles to notice body cues or becomes distressed by the focus, slow down and seek guidance. Support should always increase a sense of safety.

In the next sections, you'll explore how the sensory world affects these body signals and how to move from noticing sensations to choosing helpful regulation strategies. For now, keep it simple. The body whispers before it shouts. Teaching kids to listen to the whisper gives them a chance to respond with care.

3.2 The Sensory World: Overstimulation and Understimulation

Before we talk about coping strategies, we need to talk about the sensory world kids live in. It's louder, brighter, faster, and more demanding than many adults realize. For some children, the sensory load is like background noise they can tune out. For others, it's a constant hum that slowly drains their capacity to cope. When behavior shifts suddenly, sensory input is often part of the story.

Noise is a common trigger. A crowded room, a buzzing classroom, or a TV playing in the background while someone talks can push a child closer to overload. Clothing can do the same. A tag that scratches, a seam that rubs, socks that feel "wrong" can hijack attention and patience. Hunger and thirst lower tolerance quickly, especially in younger children whose bodies burn energy fast. Screens add another layer. Fast-moving images, sound effects, and rapid transitions can leave the nervous system revved up long after the device is turned off. Transitions themselves are sensory events too. Moving from one activity to another requires the brain and body to shift gears, which takes effort.

A vivid example comes from a three-year-old who melts down every day after daycare. The timing makes it look like a behavioral issue. When the parent looks closer, a pattern emerges. The child has been holding it together all day in a noisy, stimulating environment. By pickup, their system is spent. The meltdown is not defiance. It's release. When the parent adds a quiet snack and a few minutes of movement before any demands, the intensity drops noticeably.

Now consider an older child. A ten-year-old becomes irritable and oppositional during homework. They argue, stall, and complain. The assumption might be avoidance or attitude. But this child has been sitting still most of the day. Their body needs movement. Once the parent allows a few jumping jacks or a quick walk before starting, the resistance softens. Understimulation can look just as challenging as overstimulation.

This is where it helps to separate sensory sensitivity from emotional defiance. Sensory sensitivity means the nervous system reacts strongly to input. Emotional defiance implies a choice to oppose. When we mislabel sensory overload as defiance, we often escalate the situation. When we recognize it as a body-based need, we can respond with support instead of power struggles.

A short parent script that de-escalates without shaming might be, "Your body looks overwhelmed. Let's change the environment." This shifts the focus from behavior to support.

One practical way to support kids is by building a simple sensory menu. This is not a formal plan or a rigid schedule. It's a shared understanding of what helps your child's body settle or wake up. Movement might include stretching, jumping, or a walk. Pressure might include a hug, a heavy blanket, or squeezing a pillow. Quiet might mean dimming lights or sitting together without talking. Chewing can involve crunchy snacks or gum for older kids. Water can mean sipping, washing hands, or taking a bath. The menu grows over time as you notice what works.

You don't need to use all of these options at once. The power of a sensory menu is choice. When a child knows there are a few acceptable ways to help their body, they feel less trapped. For a six-year-old who gets wiggly at dinner, offering, "Do you want to do wall pushes or sit on a cushion?" gives agency without giving up structure.

Common mistakes can make sensory support harder. One is assuming a child should "get used to it" and ignoring discomfort.

Another is offering sensory input as a reward or threat, which turns regulation into control. A third is introducing strategies only when things are already exploding, instead of noticing patterns earlier. These missteps are understandable. They're also adjustable.

Here's a tiny practice to try today. Notice one sensory factor that seems to affect your child's mood. It might be noise, hunger, or movement. Make one small adjustment, like lowering background sound or adding a snack. Observe without expecting perfection. You're gathering information, not fixing everything.

Repair matters here too. Imagine you told your child to "stop complaining" about their clothes, and later realized the fabric really was bothering them. You can circle back and say, "I didn't listen earlier when you said your shirt was uncomfortable. I'm sorry. Let's change it now." This teaches that body signals are valid and worth respecting.

If sensory reactions are intense, persistent, or interfere significantly with daily life, additional guidance from a qualified professional can help you understand and support your child's needs more fully. Sensory awareness should make life easier, not more stressful.

3.3 From Body Clue to Regulation Plan

Noticing body sensations is only the first step. The next is helping children connect those sensations to feelings and then to coping strategies. This creates a simple, repeatable pathway: sensation leads to an emotion word, which leads to a choice that helps the body settle or focus. Over time, this pathway becomes more automatic.

For example, a child might learn that a tight belly often means worry, and that worry feels better after slow breathing or reassurance. Another child might learn that hot cheeks and clenched fists mean anger, and that anger eases with movement or squeezing something. The goal is not to eliminate feelings, but to respond to them skillfully.

A real-life example with a young child illustrates this. A four-year-old often screamed when it was time to leave the park. With support, the parent began narrating the sequence during calm times. "When it's almost time to go, your legs get jumpy and your tummy feels tight. That's your body feeling frustrated." They practiced taking three big breaths together before leaving. Over weeks, the child began to say, "My tummy's tight," and take a breath before screaming. Not every time. Enough to matter.

With an older child, the process can be more collaborative. A twelve-year-old feels overwhelmed before tests. They notice sweaty hands and a racing heart. The parent helps them connect the dots. "That body feeling often means nervous." Together, they choose strategies that fit the child, like stepping outside for fresh air or listening to music. The plan is practiced at home, not invented in the moment of panic.

Creating a personalized "My Body Map" can make this concrete. This doesn't have to be fancy. During a calm afternoon, you draw a simple outline of a body or print one. You invite your child to color or mark where they feel certain sensations. "Where do you feel excitement?" "Where does sadness show up?" You write the emotion words next to the body parts. Then you add one or two things that help in those moments, using your sensory menu as a guide. This becomes a visual reminder that the body gives clues and that there are options.

Practice during calm times is crucial. When emotions are high, the brain has less access to new learning. By rehearsing when things are steady, you increase the chances the skill will show up during storms. This practice can be brief. Five minutes is enough. The consistency matters more than the length.

A short parent script that supports this process might be, "Your body is giving us a clue. Let's check the map and choose what might help." It frames regulation as teamwork.

There are common mistakes to watch for here as well. One is rushing to strategies without naming the sensation and emotion first, which can feel dismissive. Another is insisting on a strategy the child dislikes, turning coping into compliance. A third is expecting the plan to work instantly in every situation. Regulation is a skill that develops unevenly, especially under stress.

Here's a tiny practice to try today. Pick one sensation your child experiences often, like wiggly legs or a tight belly. Together, choose one simple strategy that sometimes helps. Practice it once when your child is calm, even if there's no obvious need. This builds familiarity without pressure.

Repair continues to be part of the learning. Imagine a moment when you pushed a strategy and your child yelled, "Stop!" Later, you can say, "I tried to make you use a coping tool earlier, and that didn't feel helpful. I'm sorry. Next time, we can choose together." This restores agency and trust.

As you build regulation plans, keep expectations realistic. Some days, kids will notice early and respond smoothly. Other days, everything will fall apart anyway. Progress looks like shorter recoveries, earlier signals, and more willingness to try again.

And as always, if your child struggles to regulate despite consistent support, or if emotions and behaviors feel unsafe, seeking professional guidance can provide additional tools and reassurance. Support is not a sign that you've failed. It's part of caring for a growing nervous system.

By helping children move from body clues to thoughtful responses, you're teaching a lifelong skill. The body speaks first. Feelings follow. With practice, choice becomes possible.

Chapter 4 Co-Regulation: The Secret Superpower Parents Forget

Your calm isn't just kindness. It's biology. When children are overwhelmed, their nervous systems look for something steady to lean on. They borrow the adult nervous system until they can run their own. This is co-regulation, and it's one of the most powerful tools you have, even when it feels invisible.

Think back to the earlier chapters. You've learned to hear emotions as messages, to build a feelings dictionary, and to notice the body's early clues. Co-regulation is how all of that comes together in real time. It's what happens when your presence helps a child's racing system slow down enough for words, choices, and learning to return.

Many parents were taught that calming down is an individual task. "Go to your room and calm down." "Take a breath." Those phrases assume a skill that children are still building. Co-regulation doesn't mean fixing feelings or making them go away. It means staying close enough, steady enough, that the child's body can settle with you.

A vivid example comes from a toddler in a grocery store. The lights are bright. The cart is uncomfortable. Waiting feels endless. The child arches and screams. A parent who understands co-regulation doesn't argue or rush to explain. They lower themselves to the child's level, soften their voice, and say, "I'm here. This is a lot." The child doesn't instantly stop crying, but the intensity drops. The body has found a reference point.

Now consider an older child. A nine-year-old slams their backpack down after school and snaps at a sibling. A lecture would likely escalate things. Co-regulation looks like the parent pausing, taking one breath, and saying, "School days can be heavy. Let's slow down for a minute." The parent might sit nearby without asking questions yet. That quiet presence communicates safety more clearly than words.

This chapter invites you to see your own regulation as a gift you offer, not a performance you must perfect. You will not always feel calm. That's okay. Co-regulation works even when you're regulating yourself in front of your child. In fact, that modeling is part of the learning.

A short parent script that de-escalates without shaming might be, "I'm here with you. We'll take this one step at a time." It's simple, firm, and reassuring.

Here's a gentle practice to begin this week. Notice one moment a day when your child is mildly dysregulated, not at peak intensity. Before speaking, check your own body. Are your shoulders tight? Is your jaw clenched? Soften one place. Lower your voice slightly. Speak fewer words than you think you need. Observe what happens. You're practicing presence, not control.

If co-regulation feels unfamiliar or difficult, you're not alone. Many adults didn't receive it themselves. Learning it now can bring up strong feelings. If staying calm feels impossible or if interactions regularly escalate toward fear or harm, reaching out for professional support can help you build this skill with guidance and compassion.

4.1 What Co-Regulation Looks Like in Real Life

Co-regulation is often misunderstood as talking a lot or fixing the problem quickly. In reality, it's mostly nonverbal. Voice, pace, posture, and proximity do more to calm a child than explanations ever could.

Voice is one of the fastest regulators. A softer, slower tone sends a signal of safety. This doesn't mean whispering or sounding fake. It means dropping the volume and pace just enough to counter the child's intensity. When a child is loud and fast, your quiet and slow voice becomes an anchor.

Pace matters too. Quick movements can read as urgency or threat to an overwhelmed nervous system. Slowing down your gestures, standing still, or moving deliberately helps the child's body mirror that steadiness. Posture plays a role. An open stance, relaxed shoulders, and hands at your sides communicate availability. Looming, pointing, or crossed arms can escalate stress, even if your words are kind.

Proximity is about being close enough to be felt without crowding. Some children need a parent right beside them. Others need a bit of space with the reassurance that you're still there. You might say, "I'll sit right here," or "I'm nearby if you want a hug." Let the child's cues guide you.

A real-life example with a preschooler shows this clearly. A four-year-old throws blocks when frustrated. Instead of standing across the room and giving instructions, the parent sits on the floor a few feet away, breathes slowly, and says, "I'm here." The throwing slows. The child looks over. The parent adds, "That was really frustrating." Only after the child's body settles do they talk about what to do next.

With an older child, co-regulation can look even quieter. A twelve-year-old comes home angry after a social conflict. They don't want to talk. The parent resists the urge to question and instead offers presence. They make tea, sit at the table, and say,

"I'm around if you want company." Ten minutes later, the child begins to talk. The calm environment made space for words.

During high emotion, there's a helpful rule of thumb: less words, more presence. Explanations, lessons, and solutions land best after regulation, not during. In the heat of the moment, a few validating words and steady presence are enough. "I see how upset you are." "I'm here." Anything longer can wait.

Staying firm without escalating is part of co-regulation too. Calm doesn't mean permissive. You can hold boundaries with a steady tone and minimal language. For example, "I won't let you hit. I'm here to help you calm." Or, "It's time to leave. I'll help you walk." These scripts are short on explanation and long on containment.

Here's a vivid example with a six-year-old who refuses to leave the playground. The child screams and drops to the ground. A parent kneels nearby and says, "You're really mad about leaving." They wait a beat. "It's still time to go. I'll stay with you while your body calms." The child cries, but the parent doesn't argue or threaten. After a few minutes, the child stands up. The boundary held because the nervous system settled first.

Common mistakes can get in the way of co-regulation. One is talking too much, trying to reason a child out of a state their brain can't process. Another is matching the child's intensity with your own raised voice or sharp movements. A third is withdrawing completely, assuming the child needs to handle it alone when they actually need connection. These mistakes are understandable, especially when you're tired or triggered. Awareness gives you a chance to choose differently next time.

Here's a tiny practice to try today. Pick one phrase you'll use during big feelings, such as "I'm here," or "We'll slow this down together." Practice saying it in a calm tone when you're alone, so it comes more easily under stress. The words are simple. The practice is in how you say them.

Repair is a vital part of co-regulation. Imagine a moment when you lost your cool and raised your voice. Later, when things are calm, you might say, "Earlier I got loud when you were upset. I'm sorry. I'm still learning how to stay calm too." This repair doesn't undermine your authority. It strengthens trust and models responsibility.

Co-regulation is not about doing everything right. It's about staying connected through dysregulation and returning to steadiness together. Some days it will feel natural. Other days it will feel like work. Both are part of the process.

As you continue through this book, you'll learn how co-regulation supports boundaries and repair. For now, remember this: your calm presence is not extra. It's essential. Children learn to regulate by being regulated with. When you offer that steady ground, you're building skills that last far beyond the moment.

4.2 Repairing the Adult's Triggers

Co-regulation asks a lot of adults, not because children are doing something wrong, but because children's big feelings often brush up against our own unfinished business. A child's whining can hit an old nerve about being ignored. A public meltdown can stir shame or fear of judgment. A messy room can light up a story about respect. These are trigger loops, and they are incredibly common.

A trigger loop usually has a familiar shape. Something your child does sparks a strong reaction in you that feels bigger than the moment. Your body tightens. Your voice sharpens. You feel the urge to control, correct, or escape. The reaction happens fast because it's not just about now. It's about then. Recognizing this doesn't mean blaming your past or excusing your behavior. It means understanding what's happening so you can respond with more choice.

Picture a parent whose biggest trigger is disrespect. When their eight-year-old rolls their eyes or mutters under their breath, the parent's chest tightens. Growing up, that parent may have learned that disrespect led to harsh consequences. In the present moment, the child's behavior activates that old rule: stop this now. The reaction comes out as a raised voice or a lecture. The child reacts defensively, and the loop continues.

Or imagine a parent who feels flooded by mess. Toys everywhere feel like chaos. When their toddler dumps bins repeatedly, the parent snaps. The intensity isn't really about the toys. It's about a childhood where mess equaled criticism or a present-day life where order feels like the only control point. Seeing the loop allows space for a different response.

Separating your childhood story from your child's current behavior is a powerful step. Your child is not your parent. Your child is not testing your worth. They are learning. When you notice a trigger, you can quietly name the difference to yourself. This is now. I am the adult. My child is having a hard time, not giving me a hard time. That mental shift can soften your body enough to stay present.

Quick parent resets help interrupt trigger loops in real time. You don't need a long meditation. Sometimes ten seconds is enough. A slow breath in through the nose and out through the mouth can lower intensity. Pressing your feet into the floor and noticing the ground can bring you back into your body. Naming your own emotion silently or out loud can create distance. "I'm feeling embarrassed," or "I'm feeling overwhelmed." Naming doesn't fix the feeling, but it often reduces its grip.

A vivid example comes from a parent whose trigger is public embarrassment. Their five-year-old screams in a store. The parent feels heat rush to their face. Instead of snapping, they pause and name it internally. Embarrassed. They take one breath and say, "This is hard." Out loud to the child, they keep it simple. "I'm here. We're going to step outside." The moment isn't perfect, but it's safer.

With older kids, triggers can be subtler. A twelve-year-old's sarcasm might ignite a parent's fear of losing influence. The parent feels disrespected and wants to shut it down. Noticing the trigger allows a pause. "This is about my fear," the parent thinks, "not my child's intent." The response becomes calmer and more effective.

A short parent script that helps during a trigger might be, "I need a second to calm my body." It models self-awareness without blaming the child.

Common mistakes can make trigger repair harder. One is denying triggers exist, which leaves them running the show. Another is judging yourself harshly for having them, which adds shame. A third is expecting to eliminate triggers entirely. The goal isn't perfection. It's faster recovery and more intentional response.

Here's a tiny practice to try today. Write down one behavior that reliably gets under your skin. Next to it, jot a few words about what it brings up for you. No analysis required. Just noticing. This awareness alone can create space the next time it happens.

Repair after a hard moment is essential. Imagine you yelled when triggered by whining. Later, when things are calm, you might say, "Earlier, your whining pushed my buttons and I raised my voice. I'm sorry. I'm working on staying calm, even when it's hard." This repair doesn't excuse the behavior, but it restores connection and models accountability.

If your triggers feel overwhelming or tied to past experiences that make calm responses feel impossible, professional support can help you unpack and heal those patterns. Caring for yourself is part of caring for your child.

4.3 Boundaries Without Threats

Co-regulation does not mean letting go of limits. In fact, clear boundaries help children feel safer. The difference lies in how boundaries are held. Threats and power struggles activate fear. Calm structure activates learning.

Many adults grew up with "Because I said so" as the final word. It ended conversations, but it didn't teach skills. Replacing that phrase doesn't mean endless negotiation. It means offering a reason or a structure that respects the child's feelings while holding the line. "Because I said so" becomes "This is the rule, and I'm here to help you with it."

A boundary without threats is clear, predictable, and enforced with calm follow-through. It separates feelings from actions. A child can be furious and still not allowed to hit. A child can be sad and still expected to brush their teeth. The message is consistent: feelings are welcome; unsafe or unkind behavior is not.

Consider a toddler who throws toys when angry. A threatening response might sound like, "If you throw that again, it's gone forever." A protective boundary sounds different. The parent gets close, uses a steady voice, and says, "You're mad. I won't let you throw toys." Then they gently block the throw or move the toy. The child may cry. The boundary holds without fear.

With an older child, imagine a ten-year-old who refuses to turn off a screen and yells. A threat might escalate things. A calm boundary sounds like, "You're upset about stopping. The screen is turning off now." The parent stays nearby, ready to co-regulate. There's no lecture. The limit is enforced without humiliation.

Understanding the difference between punishment and protective limits helps here. Punishment aims to cause discomfort so behavior stops. Protective limits aim to keep everyone safe and teach what to do instead. When a child hits, a punishment might be isolation or shaming. A protective limit is blocking the hit and saying, "I won't let you hurt me. Let's find another way to show anger." The focus is safety and skill-building.

A vivid example with a preschooler illustrates this. A four-year-old bites during play. The parent feels alarmed and angry. Instead of threatening consequences in the moment, the parent intervenes physically and calmly. "I can't let you bite." They move the child to a safe space and stay present. Later, when calm, they talk about what to do when angry. The child learns that biting doesn't get needs met, but anger is still allowed.

For older kids, boundaries often involve privileges and responsibilities. A twelve-year-old breaks a family rule about respectful language. Instead of yelling, the parent says, "We speak respectfully in this house. Let's take a break and talk later." The conversation happens when both are calm. The consequence is connected to the behavior and explained without threats.

A short parent script that de-escalates while holding a boundary could be, "I hear how upset you are. This limit stays." It's firm without being cold.

Common mistakes can undermine boundaries. One is over-explaining, which can sound like negotiation during high emotion. Another is inconsistency, enforcing a rule one day and ignoring it the next, which creates confusion. A third is using boundaries to control feelings instead of actions, such as saying, "Stop being angry." These missteps are understandable and adjustable.

Here's a tiny practice to try today. Choose one boundary you enforce often. Practice saying it out loud in a calm, brief way, without adding reasons or threats. Notice how it feels in your body. Calm boundaries feel steadier, not louder.

Repair matters after boundary struggles too. Imagine you threatened a consequence out of frustration and then regretted it. Later, you might say, "Earlier I threatened something because I was overwhelmed. That wasn't the way I want to handle limits. Let's reset and be clear." This shows integrity and models repair without weakening the boundary.

Holding boundaries without threats takes practice. It asks you to trust that safety and consistency teach more than fear. Some days it will feel smooth. Other days it will feel like nothing is working. Progress looks like fewer power struggles, quicker recovery, and a growing sense of trust.

If setting boundaries feels impossible or escalates toward unsafe situations, seeking professional guidance can help you develop strategies tailored to your family. Support strengthens structure.

As you move forward, remember that co-regulation and boundaries work together. Your calm helps limits land. Clear limits help calm last. When children feel both understood and guided, they learn not just how to behave, but how to cope.

Chapter 5 Meltdowns vs. Tantrums: What's Actually Happening

There is a moment many parents recognize instantly. Your child is crying hard, maybe screaming, maybe curled on the floor or suddenly rigid and unreachable. You try to reason. You offer choices. You explain consequences. Nothing lands. The intensity only grows. In these moments, it's tempting to think, "They're doing this on purpose," or "They're trying to get their way." But here's the reframe that changes everything: a meltdown is not a negotiation. It's a nervous system overload. Treating it like defiance almost always makes it worse.

Meltdowns and tantrums can look similar on the outside. Both can involve crying, yelling, collapsing, or refusing to cooperate. The difference lives underneath. A meltdown happens when a child's system is overwhelmed beyond its capacity to cope. Control is lost. The child isn't choosing behavior in the usual sense. A tantrum, on the other hand, is often goal-driven. There is still some control, even if emotions are big. Understanding which one you're dealing with determines whether your response calms the storm or fuels it.

Picture a two-year-old in the late afternoon. They've skipped their nap, the grocery store is loud, and the line is long. When you say no to candy, they scream and drop to the floor. Their face is red, their body stiff, their cries rhythmic and panicked. This is not a child plotting manipulation. This is a nervous system that has hit its limit. Reasoning won't work because the brain systems needed for reasoning are offline. What helps here is safety, presence, and reduction of stimulation.

Now picture a seven-year-old at home who wants more screen time. When you say no, they cry loudly, glance at you, and repeat their request between sobs. When you leave the room, the crying pauses. When you return, it resumes. This child is upset, but they are also testing whether persistence will change the outcome. This is not bad or wrong. It's developmental. It's a tantrum, not a meltdown, and it calls for a different response.

Why does this distinction matter so much? Because when you treat a meltdown like a tantrum, you add pressure to an already overloaded system. You might threaten consequences or insist on compliance. The child's body hears danger and escalates further. When you treat a tantrum like a meltdown, you might over-accommodate or remove boundaries, which can unintentionally teach that intensity is the fastest path to getting needs met. Neither approach helps children build coping skills.

Timing plays a huge role in how fast kids flip. Many children unravel after school because they've spent the day holding it together. Hunger lowers tolerance. Transitions require mental and physical effort. Even positive events, like birthday parties or playdates, can lead to overload afterward. None of this means your child is fragile or spoiled. It means their system is human.

A useful way to think about these explosions is the idea of a trigger stack. Rarely does one thing cause a big reaction. More often, small stresses pile up quietly. A poor night's sleep. A rushed morning. A scratchy shirt. A difficult interaction with a friend. By the time the final trigger appears, the stack is already high. The explosion looks sudden, but the build-up has been happening all day.

A vivid example comes from a five-year-old who melts down every evening at dinner. The behavior looks dramatic and confusing. When the parent steps back and looks at the trigger stack, a pattern appears. The child skips an afternoon snack, transitions straight from noisy play to the table, and is expected to sit still after a long day. Dinner isn't the problem. It's the final straw. When the parent adds a snack, a warning before dinner, and a few minutes of movement, the meltdowns become less intense and shorter.

With older children, trigger stacks can be emotional and social. A ten-year-old who explodes over a small chore may be carrying embarrassment from school, disappointment from a canceled plan, and exhaustion from a busy schedule. The chore isn't the true cause. It's simply the moment when the system runs out of room.

A short parent script that de-escalates without shaming might be, "This looks like too much for your body right now. I'm here to help you calm." This script doesn't assume intent. It reads the situation through a nervous system lens.

Here's a small practice you can try this week. After a big reaction, wait until things are calm and then mentally rewind the day. Ask yourself what might have stacked up. Sleep, food, transitions, sensory load, social stress. You don't need to fix everything. You're learning to see patterns instead of blaming behavior.

There are common mistakes to avoid here. One is assuming all big reactions are manipulative, which leads to harsh responses. Another is assuming all big reactions are meltdowns, which can lead to removing limits unnecessarily. A third is trying to decide in the heat of the moment with certainty. Sometimes it's not clear right away. You can start with regulation and adjust later. Safety and calm are never the wrong first steps.

Repair matters after these moments too. Imagine you treated a meltdown like defiance and escalated the situation. Later, you might say, "Earlier I thought you were choosing that behavior, and I reacted strongly. Looking back, it seems like your body was overwhelmed. I'm sorry." This repair builds trust and shows your child that understanding can grow over time.

If your child's meltdowns are frequent, intense, or include safety concerns, reaching out for professional support can help you better understand their nervous system and build a plan that fits your family. Support is not a failure. It's an extension of care.

5.1 Identify the Type: Overload, Protest, or Power Struggle

Not every big reaction fits neatly into a box, but learning to identify the dominant pattern helps you respond with more confidence. Broadly speaking, intense behaviors often fall into three categories: overload, protest, or power struggle. These are not labels for children. They're lenses for adults.

Overload looks like loss of control. The child may seem unreachable. Their body is doing most of the talking. You might see shaking, screaming without clear words, hiding, or collapsing. Eye contact is minimal. The child cannot shift strategies or respond to incentives. This is the nervous system in survival mode.

Protest is different. Protest happens when a child is expressing a strong "no" to a situation they dislike. There is emotion, but there is also purpose. The child may cry, argue, or plead. They are still connected to you and to the goal of changing the outcome. Protest is healthy. It's how children practice asserting themselves.

Power struggle emerges when both adult and child dig in. The original issue becomes less important than who wins. Emotions rise on both sides. Voices get louder. The interaction turns into a tug-of-war. Power struggles are relational patterns, not character flaws. They often signal that both nervous systems need a reset.

A real-life example with a preschooler shows overload clearly. A three-year-old is asked to leave the playground. They scream, hit the ground, and cannot stand up. Offering choices or consequences does nothing. This is overload. The response is to reduce stimulation, stay close, and wait for the storm to pass.

Now a school-age example of protest. A seven-year-old is told playtime is over. They cry and say, "Just five more minutes!" They are upset but still negotiating. This is protest. You can validate the feeling and hold the boundary. "You really want more time. It's still time to go." The child may cry, but they can follow through with support.

A power struggle example might involve an eleven-year-old refusing to do homework. The parent insists. The child pushes back. The conversation spirals. Neither side is listening anymore. At this point, the issue isn't homework. It's regulation and control. Stepping back, taking a break, and returning later often does more than pushing harder.

Why do kids flip faster at certain times? After school is a classic window. Children have been managing expectations, noise, and social demands all day. Home feels safe, so emotions spill out. Hunger lowers resilience. Transitions require mental effort. Understanding these patterns doesn't mean avoiding challenges. It means timing and supporting them wisely.

The trigger stack plays a role here too. A child might start the day with a low stack and handle frustration well. On another day, the same frustration tips them into overload. When you learn to identify which type you're seeing, you stop asking the wrong question. Instead of "How do I make this stop?" you ask, "What does this nervous system need right now?"

A short parent script that fits this approach could be, "Are you overwhelmed, or are you really hoping I'll change my mind?"

You don't need an answer every time. The tone itself can slow things down.

Here's a simple practice for this section. The next time your child has a big reaction, pause and silently ask yourself which category it most resembles. Overload, protest, or power struggle. Let that guide your first move. Regulation for overload. Validation plus boundary for protest. Pause and reset for power struggle. You're building a mental habit, not following a rigid rule.

Common mistakes include trying to teach lessons during overload, backing down on limits during protest out of guilt, or doubling down during power struggles to "win." These responses are understandable. They're also opportunities to choose differently next time.

Repair is especially important when misreading the type leads to escalation. Imagine you thought your child was protesting, but they were actually overloaded. Later, you might say, "I asked you to explain when your body couldn't. Next time, I'll help you calm first." Or if you assumed overload when it was protest and removed a limit, you can repair by saying, "I see now you were upset, not overwhelmed. The rule still matters, and we can handle it together."

Learning to identify what's actually happening is a skill that grows with practice. You won't always get it right in the moment. That's okay. Each reflection builds your intuition. Over time, you'll respond with less panic and more clarity.

As you move into the next parts of this chapter, you'll learn exactly how to respond to meltdowns and how to prevent some of them before they start. For now, remember this: behavior is communication filtered through a nervous system. When you understand the system, your responses become calmer, kinder, and more effective.

5.2 The Melt-Down Response Plan (Step-by-Step)

When a true meltdown is underway, the goal is not to teach a lesson or win cooperation. The goal is to help a flooded nervous system find safety again. Think of this as first aid for emotions. You don't ask someone with a bleeding cut to explain what happened before you apply pressure. You stabilize first. Teaching comes later.

Safety comes first, and safety is broader than it sounds. It includes physical safety, like preventing hitting or running into the street, and sensory safety, like reducing noise, lights, or crowding. If a child is thrashing, you may need to move nearby objects or guide their body away from danger. This can be done calmly and firmly. "I won't let you hurt yourself. I'm here." The tone matters as much as the action.

Reducing stimulation often brings the fastest relief. That might mean stepping into a quieter space, dimming lights, turning off background noise, or creating a small boundary with your body to block visual chaos. A three-year-old melting down at a birthday party may calm faster outside with you than in the middle of the room. A nine-year-old overwhelmed after school may need shoes off, backpack down, and silence before any questions. You're not rewarding behavior. You're helping a nervous system reset.

Simplifying choices helps too. During overload, the brain cannot process options. "Do you want the red cup or the blue cup?" can feel like pressure. Fewer words, fewer decisions. You might say, "We're going to sit here and breathe," or "I'm going to hold your hand and keep you safe." This reduces demand when capacity is low.

Regulation comes before teaching, always. Lectures during meltdowns don't work because the parts of the brain that learn are offline. Your job is to co-regulate. Use your body as a guide. Slow your breathing so your child can match it. Lower your voice. Keep your face soft. Stay present. You can name what you see without analysis. "Your body is having a big wave." "This feels like too much." These statements don't ask for anything. They reassure.

A vivid example with a preschooler makes this concrete. A four-year-old screams and throws shoes when it's time to leave a playdate. The parent kneels, blocks the throw, and says, "I won't let you throw shoes. I'm here." They guide the child to a quiet hallway, sit together, and breathe. There's no explanation yet. After a few minutes, the screaming slows. Only then does the parent add, "Leaving was really hard." The child nods. Regulation opened the door.

With an older child, the approach is similar, though the form changes. A ten-year-old collapses into tears over homework. The parent resists the urge to explain deadlines and instead sits nearby. "This is overwhelming. I'm with you." They offer a glass of water and wait. When the child's breathing slows, the parent asks one gentle question. "Do you want a break or help starting?" Teaching comes after calm returns.

Aftercare matters just as much as the moment itself. Once everyone is regulated, you reconnect. You don't shame or replay every detail. You name what happened simply. "Earlier, your body got really overwhelmed when it was time to leave." You validate without excusing unsafe behavior. "That was hard. Throwing shoes isn't okay." Then you plan one small tweak for next time. "Next time, we'll use a five-minute warning and bring a snack." One tweak is enough. More can overwhelm.

A short parent script that de-escalates without shaming might be, "This is a meltdown, not a choice. I'm here to help you through it." It frames the response with compassion and clarity.

Common mistakes can creep in, especially under stress. One is trying to reason too soon, which adds fuel to the fire. Another is taking the behavior personally and escalating emotionally. A third is withdrawing completely, leaving the child alone before they have the skills to self-regulate. These are understandable reactions. Noticing them helps you choose differently next time.

Here's a tiny practice to try today. Pick one phrase you'll use during meltdowns, such as "I'm here," or "We'll get through this." Practice saying it slowly when you're calm. Repetition builds muscle memory for hard moments.

Repair after a hard moment strengthens trust. Imagine you raised your voice during a meltdown. Later, when calm, you might say, "Earlier, I got loud when your body was overwhelmed. I wish I had stayed calmer. I'm sorry." This repair doesn't erase the boundary. It repairs the connection and models responsibility.

If meltdowns involve frequent safety risks, last a long time, or feel unmanageable despite support, it's wise to seek professional guidance. Extra help can tailor strategies to your child's nervous system and your family's context.

5.3 Preventing the Next One

Not all meltdowns can be prevented, and that's okay. Children are growing nervous systems, not machines. Still, many meltdowns can be softened or shortened by changing what happens before the tipping point. Prevention is about building predictability, teaching early requests for help, and tracking patterns with curiosity rather than blame.

Predictable routines create a sense of safety that lowers baseline stress. When children know what comes next, their bodies don't have to stay on high alert. This doesn't mean rigid schedules. It means reliable rhythms. Morning routines that follow the same general order. After-school decompression time before homework. Bedtime cues that signal winding down. Predictability frees up energy for coping.

Warning systems help with transitions, which are common triggers. Timers, verbal countdowns, and simple scripts prepare the nervous system. A parent might say, "Five more minutes, then we clean up," and repeat it once. Or, "After this episode, screens are done." The key is consistency and calm delivery. The warning works best when it's followed through, even when feelings are big.

Teaching kids to request breaks before they explode is a powerful prevention tool. This skill grows from the body awareness you practiced in earlier chapters. You might teach a simple phrase like, "I need a break," or a signal like holding up a hand. Practice it during calm times. Praise the request when it happens, even if you can't fully meet it in that moment. "Thanks for telling me early. Let's take one minute."

A vivid example with a school-age child shows this in action. An eight-year-old often melts down during homework. Together, parent and child practice noticing early signs, like a tight belly or fast breathing. They agree on a signal: tapping the desk. One afternoon, the child taps instead of exploding. The parent responds, "I see your signal. Let's take a quick break." The meltdown doesn't disappear forever, but its intensity drops over time.

Tracking patterns like a scientist helps you adjust without judgment. Instead of asking, "What's wrong with my child?" you ask, "What conditions make things harder?" Look at sleep, food, screen time, and social load. A late bedtime might correlate with morning meltdowns. Too much screen time might lead to irritability. A busy weekend might make Monday harder. You don't need a chart on the wall. A few mental notes are enough.

With younger children, prevention might look like adding a snack before errands or scheduling errands earlier in the day. With older children, it might involve building in quiet time after social events or limiting commitments during stressful weeks. These adjustments are not indulgent. They're supportive.

A short parent script that supports prevention without shame could be, "Let's plan for your body, not fight it." This frames accommodations as wise, not weak.

Common mistakes in prevention include expecting routines to eliminate all meltdowns, overloading children with warnings and reminders, or using prevention tools as threats. Another mistake is tracking patterns to prove a point rather than to understand. Curiosity works better than criticism.

Here's a tiny practice to try today. Think of one predictable meltdown window, like after school or before dinner. Add one small support there, such as a snack, quiet time, or a clear warning. Observe what changes, without expecting perfection.

Repair after missed prevention is just as important. Imagine you skipped the warning and a meltdown followed. Later, you can say, "I didn't give you a heads-up before we switched activities. That made it harder. Next time, I'll try to warn you." This shows accountability and reinforces learning.

As you work on prevention, remember that flexibility is part of the plan. What helps one month may not help the next as children grow and circumstances change. Stay curious. Adjust gently. Celebrate small shifts, like earlier signals or quicker recovery.

If prevention strategies don't seem to help and meltdowns remain intense or frequent, additional support can offer fresh eyes and tailored ideas. Parenting deeply feeling kids is demanding work. You don't have to do it alone.

Meltdowns are not failures. They are signals. When you respond with safety in the moment and curiosity afterward, you teach children that even big storms can be weathered together. Over time, that knowledge becomes a source of resilience that reaches far beyond childhood.

Chapter 6 Big Feelings: Anger, Frustration, and Aggression

Anger gets a bad reputation in families. It's loud. It's uncomfortable. It can look scary, especially when it shows up as yelling, throwing, or hitting. But anger is often a bodyguard emotion. It steps in to protect something softer underneath, like hurt, fear, disappointment, or shame. When we treat anger as the enemy, children learn to hide what's really going on. When we treat anger as a signal, children learn to tell the truth about their inner world.

You've already built important foundations in earlier chapters. You've learned to name feelings, read body cues, co-regulate, and respond to meltdowns with safety. This chapter builds on that work by focusing on anger specifically, because anger is one of the most misunderstood emotions in childhood. It's also one of the most useful, when handled with care.

Consider a common scene with a young child. A three-year-old grabs a toy from a sibling and hits when the sibling protests. The hitting gets all the attention. It's easy to label the child as aggressive or "mean." But when you slow the moment down, a different story often appears. The child wanted connection, control, or fairness. They didn't have words. Anger rushed in to protect that need. If we only address the hitting, we miss the chance to teach what anger is guarding.

Now picture an older child. A ten-year-old comes home from school furious and snaps at everyone. When asked what's wrong, they shout, "Nothing!" The anger feels outsized compared to what you can see. Later, you learn they were excluded from a group at recess. The anger wasn't random. It was protecting hurt and embarrassment. Without support, anger becomes the only language available.

Anger itself is not dangerous. What children do with anger can be. That's an important distinction. The goal is not to eliminate anger or demand calm at all costs. The goal is to help children understand what anger is telling them and to express it safely. When children feel shamed for being angry, they either suppress it or explode later. When they feel guided, they gain options.

A short parent script that de-escalates without shaming might be, "I see how angry you are. Let's figure out what it's protecting." This communicates curiosity instead of fear or control.

Here's a simple practice you can start this week. The next time your child shows anger, even in a mild way, pause before correcting the behavior. Name the anger neutrally. "That's anger." Then add a wondering statement. "I wonder what's underneath." You don't need an answer right away. You're planting the idea that anger has meaning.

As always, if anger regularly turns into unsafe behavior or feels overwhelming for you or your child, professional support can help you build strategies that fit your family. Seeking help is a sign of care, not failure.

6.1 The Anger Iceberg: What's Under the Surface

An iceberg is a helpful image for understanding anger. What we see above the water is the visible behavior: yelling, stomping, hitting, slamming doors. What sits below the surface is often much larger and quieter: sadness, fear, jealousy, shame, grief, or feeling powerless. Children are rarely taught to look below the surface. They need guidance to do that safely.

Helping kids identify what's under their anger starts with slowing the moment down. This doesn't happen in the peak of a rage. It happens during calmer times or in the aftercare that follows. You might say, "Earlier you were really angry. Sometimes anger shows up when something else hurts. Let's see if we can find it." This frames exploration as a shared task, not an interrogation.

A vivid example with a preschooler shows how this works. A five-year-old screams and throws markers when their drawing doesn't look right. In the moment, the parent focuses on safety and co-regulation. Later, when calm, the parent sits with the child and says, "When the picture didn't turn out how you wanted, you got really mad." The child nods. The parent continues, "Sometimes that kind of mad is protecting a sad feeling. Does that fit?" The child shrugs, then quietly says, "I wanted it to be good." Beneath the anger was disappointment and fear of not being good enough. Naming that reduces the need for anger to shout.

With older children, the iceberg can be more complex. A twelve-year-old snaps angrily when asked about homework. The parent senses resistance and irritation. Instead of pushing, they wait until later and say, "When I asked about homework, you got really angry. I'm wondering if there was something underneath, like worry or feeling stuck." The child hesitates, then admits they're afraid of failing. Anger was protecting fear. Once the fear is named, collaboration becomes possible.

Language plays a key role here. Teaching children to use "I feel... because... I need..." gives them a structure for honesty. This is not a script they must recite perfectly. It's a scaffold you model and practice gently. For a young child, it might sound like, "I feel mad because my tower fell. I need help." For an older child, it might be, "I feel angry because I felt left out. I need some space." The power of this language is that it connects feeling to cause and need, without blame.

Reducing shame is essential for this work. Many children believe that certain feelings make them bad. Anger, jealousy, and shame itself often fall into this category. When children sense judgment, they protect themselves by denying or escalating. You can reduce shame by normalizing the experience. "Lots of kids feel angry when that happens." Or, "That feeling makes sense." This doesn't mean agreeing with behavior. It means making feelings safe to discuss.

A real-life example highlights the importance of shame reduction. A seven-year-old hits a peer at school and comes home angry and defensive. The parent resists the urge to lecture and instead says, "Hitting isn't okay, and I want to understand what led up to it." The child eventually admits they were embarrassed after being laughed at. The anger was armor. When the parent responds with empathy for the embarrassment while still holding the boundary about hitting, the child is more willing to learn alternatives.

A short parent script that supports this exploration might be, "Anger usually has a reason. We can look for it together." It's simple and reassuring.

There are common mistakes to avoid when working with the anger iceberg. One is trying to dig for hidden feelings too aggressively, which can feel invasive. Another is assuming you know what's underneath without asking, which can make children feel misunderstood. A third is minimizing the softer feelings once they appear, saying things like, "That's not a big deal." These responses can shut down honesty. Patience and curiosity work better.

Here's a tiny practice to try today. During a calm moment, share an age-appropriate example of your own anger iceberg. You might say, "I was angry earlier when the meeting ran late. Underneath, I think I was worried about missing time with you." This models reflection without burdening your child.

Repair after a hard moment is especially important with anger. Imagine you responded harshly to your child's anger and later realized you missed what was underneath. You can circle back and say, "Earlier I focused on stopping the yelling and didn't listen enough. I'm sorry. If you want, we can talk about what you were feeling." This repair restores trust and shows that understanding can grow after mistakes.

As you continue into the next sections of this chapter, you'll learn how to help children release anger safely and how to teach conflict skills early. For now, hold onto this idea: anger is information. When children learn to look beneath it, they gain access to their real needs. And when you help them do that with compassion and structure, you're teaching a skill that will serve them long after childhood.

6.2 Safe Anger Release (Without Breaking Things or People)

Once children begin to understand that anger is a signal and not a character flaw, the next question naturally follows: what do we do with it? Anger is energy. When it has nowhere safe to go, it spills out sideways, often toward people or objects that don't deserve it. Teaching children how to release anger safely is one of the most practical skills you can offer, and it starts with permission. Not permission to hurt, but permission to feel and move.

Safe anger release is especially important for kids whose bodies fill quickly with intensity. A child who clenches their fists, stomps, or growls is not being dramatic. Their nervous system is mobilized. Trying to talk them out of that energy rarely works. Giving the body a way to discharge it does.

Physical outlets are often the most effective place to start. A six-year-old who wants to hit can push hard against a wall with their palms. A four-year-old can stomp their feet like a dinosaur. An eight-year-old can squeeze a stress ball or rip paper into tiny pieces. An older child might carry something heavy, do slow squats, or take a brisk walk. These actions meet anger where it lives, in the body, without causing harm.

A vivid example comes from a preschooler who frequently hit when frustrated. Instead of only saying "no hitting," the parent introduced wall pushes during calm times. They practiced together, laughing at first. When anger showed up later, the parent blocked the hit and said, "Hands go on the wall." The child pushed hard, grunted, and then melted into tears. The anger moved through instead of turning outward.

With older children, safe release can look quieter. A ten-year-old who slams doors when angry might be offered a heavy pillow to punch or a notebook to scribble furiously. A twelve-year-old might need space to pace or music to move to. The form matters less than the principle: anger needs a safe outlet.

This is where "anger rules" for the home can be helpful, as long as they're framed with respect. Anger rules are simple agreements about where, when, and how anger can be expressed safely. You might say, "In our house, you can be angry anywhere, but you can't hurt people or break things." Then you add, "Here are the things you can do when anger shows up." These agreements are best introduced during calm moments, not in the heat of conflict.

Stopping aggression without escalating is a skill worth practicing. When a child moves toward hitting, yelling, or throwing, your response needs to be quick, clear, and calm. Long explanations often add fuel. Short phrases paired with action work better. "I won't let you hit," said while gently blocking the arm. "I'm moving this away to keep everyone safe," said while removing an object. The tone is firm but not angry. The goal is containment, not punishment.

A real-life example with a school-age child shows this balance. An eight-year-old throws a book in anger. The parent steps in, picks up the book, and says, "I won't let you throw things." They stay nearby and add, "You can stomp or squeeze this instead." The child protests at first, then stomps hard. The aggression stops because the energy found a safer path.

A short parent script that de-escalates without shaming might be, "Anger is okay. Hurting is not. I'll help you find another way." This sentence separates feeling from action and communicates support.

Common mistakes can make anger release harder. One is allowing unsafe venting, like hitting pillows near people or throwing objects that can still scare others. Another is shaming physical release by calling it "bad behavior" even when it's safe. A third is introducing outlets only after aggression has already escalated, rather than practicing them ahead of time. These mistakes are understandable. Adjusting them takes awareness, not perfection.

Here's a tiny practice to try today. During a calm moment, ask your child to choose one safe anger outlet they're willing to try. Practice it together for thirty seconds. Keep it light. The goal is familiarity, not mastery.

Repair after a hard moment is especially important with anger. Imagine your child hit and you reacted sharply. Later, you might say, "Earlier, I focused on stopping the hitting, and I didn't help you release the anger safely. I'm sorry. Next time, we'll try one of our anger tools." This repair doesn't excuse aggression. It restores teamwork.

If anger frequently turns into aggression that feels hard to contain, or if you're worried about safety, reaching out for professional support can help you create a plan that fits your child's needs. Getting help is part of protecting everyone involved.

6.3 Teaching Conflict Skills Early

Anger often shows up in the middle of conflict. Siblings argue. Friends disappoint each other. Boundaries clash. Children are not born knowing how to disagree respectfully. They learn by watching, practicing, and being coached in real time. Teaching conflict skills early doesn't prevent all fights, but it gives children tools to repair and move forward.

The first step is modeling. Children absorb how adults handle disagreement. When you say, "I don't like that," instead of using insults or sarcasm, you're showing that it's possible to express displeasure without attacking. When you narrate your own conflict calmly, you teach more than any lecture. "I'm frustrated because the plan changed. I'm going to take a breath and think."

With young children, modeling happens in simple language. A parent might say to a toddler sibling, "I don't like when you grab. I'm using this." The words are basic, but the structure is powerful. It names the problem without labeling the child.

For school-age kids, modeling can be more explicit. When a child complains about a peer, you might say, "Let's practice what you could say. Instead of 'You're mean,' you could say, 'I didn't like that.'" Practicing this outside the heat of the moment builds confidence.

Roleplay is one of the most effective ways to rehearse conflict skills. It doesn't have to be formal or serious. You can use toys, drawings, or silly voices. A parent might say, "Let's pretend I took your toy. What could you say?" The child tries a response. You adjust gently. "That gets your point across. Let's try it with a calmer voice." Roleplay makes the unfamiliar familiar.

Teaching a simple problem-solving flow helps older children move beyond blame. You define the problem together. You brainstorm options, even silly ones. You choose one to try. You check back later to see how it went. This doesn't need to be labeled or structured rigidly. It can sound like, "So the problem is both of you want the same game. What are some ideas?" The process matters more than the solution.

A vivid example with siblings illustrates this. Two siblings fight over a game and start yelling. After calming down, the parent sits with them and says, "Let's figure this out. What's the problem?"

Each child shares. The parent reflects and asks for ideas. They agree to take turns. Later, the parent checks in. "How did that plan work?" The conflict becomes a learning moment instead of a power struggle.

With older children, conflict skills extend to friendships and school. A twelve-year-old feels angry at a friend who canceled plans. Instead of sending a harsh text, the parent helps them draft a message. "I felt disappointed when plans changed. Can we reschedule?" This models directness without aggression.

A short parent script that supports this learning might be, "Let's say what you didn't like without hurting." It's a simple reminder of the goal.

Common mistakes can undermine conflict teaching. One is stepping in too quickly and solving the problem for the child, which robs them of practice. Another is expecting children to use skills perfectly under stress without rehearsal. A third is focusing only on fairness instead of emotional impact. These mistakes are natural. Noticing them helps you shift toward coaching.

Here's a tiny practice to try today. Choose a low-stakes disagreement, perhaps over a toy or turn. Guide your child to use one respectful phrase, like "I don't like that." Praise the effort, not the outcome. Skill-building takes time.

Repair after conflict is a critical part of learning. Imagine you jumped in angrily during a sibling fight. Later, you can say, "I got loud when you were arguing. I wish I had helped you practice your words instead. Let's try again next time." This shows that even adults are learning conflict skills.

Teaching conflict skills early doesn't mean expecting children to be calm all the time. It means giving them language and structure they can grow into. Some days they'll remember. Other days they won't. What matters is that the skills are there, waiting to be used.

If conflicts in your home regularly escalate into fear or harm, or if your child struggles to use any of these skills despite support, professional guidance can help you tailor strategies and ensure safety. Support strengthens learning.

Anger and conflict are part of being human. When children learn how to release anger safely and handle conflict with words instead of wounds, they're not just becoming easier to live with. They're becoming more capable, connected, and confident in navigating relationships for the rest of their lives.

Chapter 7 Anxiety and Worry: Helping Kids Feel Safe in an Uncertain World

Kids don't need a life without fear. They need a brain that learns, again and again, "I can handle fear." That distinction matters. Fear is part of being human. It shows up when something is new, uncertain, or important. Trying to eliminate fear teaches children to avoid life. Teaching them how to meet fear with support teaches resilience.

Anxiety often sneaks into family life quietly. It can look like endless questions, refusal to try new things, sudden irritability, or complaints about aches that don't seem to have a clear cause. Parents may feel torn between wanting to protect their child from discomfort and wanting them to grow. This chapter begins by easing that tension. You don't need to choose between comfort and courage. You can build both, together.

Think of a five-year-old who suddenly refuses to go to birthday parties. Last year they loved them. This year they cling to your leg and cry before you even reach the door. Or imagine a ten-year-old who erases homework repeatedly, desperate for it to be perfect, and melts down when it's time to turn it in. Or a seven-year-old who complains of a stomachache every school morning and feels fine by mid-afternoon. These are not random behaviors. They are signals from a nervous system that's trying to stay safe.

Modern childhood adds layers of uncertainty that previous generations didn't face in the same way. Performance pressure starts earlier. Screens bring constant comparison and stimulation. News and adult conversations seep into young ears. Social dynamics can be relentless, even in elementary school. Children don't always have words for this, but their bodies and behaviors tell the story.

Anxiety doesn't mean something is wrong with your child or your parenting. It means your child's brain is highly tuned to potential threats and hasn't yet learned how to turn the alarm down. Your role is not to argue with the alarm or make promises you can't keep. Your role is to help your child feel safe enough to practice handling the alarm when it goes off.

A short parent script that de-escalates without shaming might be, "Your worry is trying to protect you. I'm here to help you handle it." This acknowledges the fear without letting it take control.

Here's a gentle practice you can try this week. When your child shares a worry, resist the urge to immediately reassure or fix. Instead, reflect first. "That sounds scary." Pause. Let the feeling land. Often, being heard reduces the intensity enough for the next step. You're teaching your child that fear can be spoken out loud and survived.

As with every chapter, it's important to say this clearly. If anxiety significantly interferes with your child's daily life, leads to extreme avoidance, or is paired with safety concerns, professional support can be very helpful. Asking for help is a way of expanding your child's support system, not a sign that you've failed.

7.1 The Many Faces of Anxiety

Anxiety rarely announces itself clearly. It wears many disguises, especially in children. Some kids share worry thoughts openly. Others show anxiety through behavior or physical symptoms. Learning to recognize these different faces helps you respond with understanding instead of confusion or frustration.

Worry thoughts are the most obvious form. These might sound like "What if I mess up?" "What if you forget me?" or "What if something bad happens?" Younger children may repeat the same questions over and over, not because they didn't hear the answer, but because their nervous system is seeking safety. Older children may keep worries inside, ruminating quietly.

Avoidance is another common face of anxiety. A child avoids trying out for the team, going to a sleepover, or even answering questions in class. Avoidance can look like laziness or defiance on the surface, but underneath it's often fear of discomfort, embarrassment, or failure. When avoidance works, meaning it reduces anxiety in the short term, the brain learns to rely on it. That's why it can become so sticky.

Perfectionism is anxiety wearing a socially acceptable mask. A child who must get everything exactly right may appear driven or mature, but the inner experience is often tense and fragile. Mistakes feel threatening, not instructive. The child isn't chasing excellence. They're running from fear.

Physical symptoms are especially common in younger kids. Stomachaches, headaches, nausea, or sudden fatigue can all be expressions of anxiety. This doesn't mean the pain isn't real. The body is doing exactly what it's designed to do when it senses threat. When stress hormones rise, digestion and comfort change. Listening to these signals with curiosity helps children feel believed and supported.

Irritability is another overlooked sign. An anxious child may snap, argue, or melt down over small things. Living with constant internal tension is exhausting. When the system is stretched thin, patience runs out faster.

A vivid example comes from a six-year-old who becomes aggressive during morning routines. They yell and refuse to get dressed. The behavior seems oppositional until the parent notices a pattern. The child's stomach hurts on school days. When asked gently, the child admits they're worried about reading aloud in class. The anger in the morning is covering fear. Once the fear is named, mornings become a place for support instead of battles.

With older children, anxiety can look quieter. A twelve-year-old spends hours rechecking assignments and panics about grades. When a parent responds with "You're doing great, stop worrying," the anxiety doesn't ease. When the parent says, "It sounds like you're scared of disappointing people," the child finally exhales. Being seen is regulating.

One area that often confuses parents is the difference between anxiety and excitement. Both can come with butterflies, fast heartbeats, and restless energy. The difference often lies in the child's thoughts and behavior. Excitement pulls a child toward something. Anxiety pushes them away. A child who is excited might say, "I'm nervous, but I want to try." A child who is anxious might say, "I can't do it," or avoid entirely. Helping children notice this difference builds self-awareness without labeling them.

Modern triggers deserve special attention. Performance pressure shows up in academics, sports, and even social situations. Screens can amplify comparison and reduce downtime, making nervous systems more reactive. News and adult conversations about danger or uncertainty can plant worry seeds that children don't know how to process. Social dynamics, especially exclusion or online interactions, can feel relentless. None of this means screens or activities are inherently bad. It means children need help metabolizing what they take in.

A short parent script that helps clarify anxiety without shaming might be, "This sounds like worry trying to keep you safe. Let's listen to it without letting it decide everything." It validates the feeling while gently separating it from action.

Common mistakes can unintentionally feed anxiety. One is dismissing worries with "You're fine," which can make children feel alone with their fear. Another is over-reassuring, answering the same question endlessly, which can strengthen the anxiety loop. A third is labeling children as "anxious" in a way that feels fixed or defining. These mistakes are understandable. Awareness helps you shift.

Here's a tiny practice to try today. When your child shows a sign of anxiety, name the pattern instead of the problem. You might say, "I notice your stomach hurts when it's time for school," or "I see you erasing a lot." Then pause. Let your child add meaning. This invites reflection instead of defense.

Repair after a hard moment matters here too. Imagine you brushed off a worry because you were tired or rushed. Later, you can say, "Earlier, I didn't slow down when you shared your worry. I'm sorry. I want to understand." This repair teaches your child that worries are worth attention, even if the timing isn't always perfect.

As you move through this chapter, keep in mind that anxiety is not a verdict about the future. It's a signal about the present. With support, children learn that fear can show up without taking over. In the next sections, you'll learn specific tools to help children build courage gently and create routines that make safety feel more predictable. For now, start with recognition. When you can see anxiety clearly, you can respond with steadiness instead of fear.

7.2 Courage Tools That Actually Work

When anxiety shows up, many parents instinctively reach for reassurance. "It'll be fine." "Don't worry." "Nothing bad will happen." These words come from love, but they often don't stick. Anxiety isn't a logic problem. It's a safety problem. Courage tools work not because they erase fear, but because they teach the brain, through experience, "I can feel this and still cope."

One of the most effective tools for anxious kids is something called contained worry. Instead of trying to stop worry altogether, you give it a small, predictable space. This is often called "worry time." The idea is simple and surprisingly calming. Worries are welcome, but not all day long. They have a place.

For a younger child, worry time might be five minutes before dinner. You sit together and say, "This is worry time. You can tell me any worries your brain has." You listen without fixing. When time is up, you gently close it. "Worry time is done. If worries pop up later, we'll save them for tomorrow." Over time, many children worry less because the brain learns it doesn't need to shout all day to be heard.

With an older child, worry time can be more collaborative. A ten-year-old who constantly asks "what if" questions might agree to write worries down and bring them to a set time. This doesn't make you unavailable. It makes you predictable. Predictability is calming to an anxious brain.

Another tool that actually works is exposure in tiny steps. Exposure sounds intimidating, but it doesn't mean throwing kids into the deep end. It means helping them approach what they fear in manageable pieces, with support. Avoidance teaches the brain that fear is dangerous. Gentle exposure teaches the brain that fear rises and falls.

Consider a six-year-old who refuses to sleep alone. Instead of insisting they stay in their room all night or letting them move into your bed indefinitely, you might create a gradual plan. The first step could be sitting on the bed until they fall asleep. The next step might be sitting in a chair nearby. Later, sitting outside the door. Each step is practiced until the child's body adjusts. The goal isn't zero fear. It's tolerable fear with success.

With older kids, exposure might involve social situations or performance. A twelve-year-old terrified of speaking in class might start by reading one sentence aloud at home, then to you, then to a trusted friend, then to a small group. Each step builds evidence. "I felt scared, and I got through it."

Cognitive tools can also help, especially when paired with warmth and play. Thought bubbles work well for younger children. You draw a bubble and say, "This is a worry thought." You draw another and say, "This is a helper thought." You don't argue with the worry. You compare. "The worry says, 'I'll mess up.' The helper says, 'I can try even if it's not perfect.'" The child begins to see thoughts as messages, not commands.

Some children like externalizing worry through characters. A worry monster, worry bug, or worry cloud can carry the fear so it doesn't feel like the child's identity. A parent might say, "It sounds like the worry monster is loud today." This creates distance without dismissal. Older children may prefer more direct language, like asking, "Is this a fact or a fear?" Facts are what we know for sure. Fears are predictions. Learning the difference builds mental flexibility.

A vivid example comes from an eight-year-old who panics before soccer practice. The parent sits with them and draws two circles. One says "Facts." One says "Fears." Together they sort thoughts. "Coach will be there" goes in facts. "Everyone will laugh at me" goes in fears. The fear doesn't disappear, but it loses authority. The child goes to practice feeling scared and capable.

A short parent script that de-escalates without shaming might be, "We're not trying to make the worry go away. We're teaching you how to carry it." This reframes courage as skill-building, not toughness.

Common mistakes can get in the way of courage tools. One is moving too fast, pushing children past what they can handle, which teaches the brain that fear really is dangerous. Another is rescuing too quickly, removing all discomfort, which teaches the brain that fear must be avoided. A third is debating worries with logic alone, which often increases anxiety. Courage grows in the space between pressure and protection.

Here's a tiny practice to try today. Help your child name one worry and rate how big it feels on a scale of one to ten. Then ask, "What's one tiny step we could take that would make it a nine instead of a ten?" Keep the step small. Celebrate the trying, not the outcome.

Repair matters when courage plans misfire. Imagine you pushed your child to do something and they panicked. Later, you can say, "I asked you to take a step that was too big. I'm sorry. Let's slow it down and try again together." This teaches that bravery is adjustable, not all-or-nothing.

If anxiety feels entrenched, exposure feels impossible, or fear is shrinking your child's world significantly, professional support can help guide these steps safely. Courage tools work best when they're matched to the child's capacity.

7.3 Creating a Safety-First Routine

While courage tools help children face fear, routines help reduce how often fear shows up. An anxious brain scans constantly for uncertainty. Predictable rhythms tell the brain, "You are safe enough to rest." This doesn't mean life becomes rigid or boring. It means the basics are reliable.

Sleep is one of the strongest foundations for anxiety. A tired brain has less flexibility and more alarm. Consistent bedtimes, even on weekends when possible, support emotional regulation. This doesn't require perfection. It requires a general rhythm the body can count on.

Nutrition and movement matter too. Hunger can mimic anxiety, and regular meals stabilize energy. Movement helps burn off stress hormones and settle the nervous system. For some kids, quiet movement like stretching or walking is calming. For others, active play is necessary before calm can arrive. Watching your child helps you choose.

Predictability also comes from routines around transitions. Morning routines that follow the same order. After-school routines that include decompression. Bedtime routines that signal winding down. These routines don't eliminate anxiety, but they lower the background noise so worries don't have to shout as loudly.

Bedtime deserves special attention. Many children's worries grow louder in the dark, when distractions fade. Calm bedtime scripts can help. A parent might say, "Your job is to rest. My job is to keep you safe." Or, "Even if worries come, your body knows how to sleep." These scripts aren't magic spells. They're steady reminders.

Body-based wind-down strategies often work better than talking at night. Gentle stretching, slow breathing together, listening to calm music, or a warm bath can cue the nervous system toward rest. Some children like pressure, like a weighted blanket or a long hug. Others prefer space. Let your child's preferences guide you.

Reassurance seeking is one of the trickiest parts of anxiety for parents. Children ask the same questions over and over because reassurance gives short-term relief. Unfortunately, it can feed the anxiety loop long-term. The goal is not to refuse reassurance harshly, but to respond in a way that builds independence.

Instead of answering every "Are you sure?" with a new explanation, you might offer a consistent response. "I've answered that, and I believe you can handle the worry." Or, "That's a worry question. What does your brave brain say?" This gently shifts responsibility back to the child without abandonment.

A vivid example comes from a nine-year-old who asks every night if the doors are locked. The parent initially checks repeatedly. The anxiety grows. When the parent changes approach, they check once together and say, "The doors are locked. If the worry asks again, remind it we already checked." The child still worries, but over time the questions decrease. The brain learns to tolerate uncertainty.

A short parent script that supports safety without feeding the loop might be, "I know you want reassurance. I trust you to use your tools." It's calm, confident, and non-shaming.

Common mistakes in routines include becoming overly rigid, which can backfire when plans change, or treating routines as rewards or punishments. Another mistake is responding to reassurance seeking with irritation, which can increase anxiety. Gentle consistency works better than emotional reactions.

Here's a tiny practice to try today. Choose one part of your day that often feels rushed or tense. Add one predictable element, like the same song, phrase, or order of events. Notice how your child responds over the next few days.

Repair after routine breakdowns matters too. Imagine a chaotic morning where everything went off track and anxiety spiked. Later, you can say, "This morning was messy, and that made worries louder. Tomorrow, we'll try to get back to our rhythm." This normalizes disruption without blame.

As you bring courage tools and safety-first routines together, remember that progress is uneven. Some weeks will feel easier. Others will feel heavy. What matters is the message you're sending over time: fear can be felt, named, and handled within connection.

If anxiety continues to dominate daily life despite consistent routines and tools, or if your child's fear feels too big for either of you to manage safely, professional support can offer relief and guidance. You don't have to carry this alone.

Children don't need certainty to thrive. They need enough safety, structure, and support to discover their own courage. When you build routines that steady the nervous system and tools that invite bravery, you're helping your child grow a quiet, powerful belief: "I can handle what comes."

Chapter 8 Sadness, Grief, and Disappointment: Letting Feelings Move Through

When sadness is allowed, it softens. When it's rushed, it hardens into anger, numbness, or shutdown. This chapter is about making room for the quieter emotions that often get overlooked in family life. Sadness doesn't shout like anger or demand like anxiety. It whispers. And because it whispers, adults often feel tempted to fix it quickly or cheer it away.

You've already spent weeks learning how to name feelings, read body cues, co-regulate, and handle big storms. Sadness asks for a slightly different posture. It asks for patience, stillness, and trust in the process. Children don't need sadness erased. They need sadness accompanied.

Picture a four-year-old whose balloon pops at a party. The tears come fast, then turn into sobs that seem bigger than the moment. An adult instinctively says, "It's okay, we'll get another one!" The intention is kind, but the message can land as, "Stop feeling this." The sadness has nowhere to go, so it often comes back later as irritability or aggression.

Now picture a nine-year-old who doesn't make the team they hoped for. They come home quiet, retreat to their room, and don't want dinner. An adult worries and pushes conversation or positivity. "You'll do better next time." "At least you tried." The child nods but feels unseen. The disappointment settles deeper, sometimes showing up days later as anger or withdrawal.

Sadness is part of being human. It signals loss, endings, unmet hopes, and change. When children learn that sadness can be felt fully and safely, they gain emotional flexibility. They learn that feelings move. They don't get stuck forever.

This chapter focuses on letting sadness move through instead of around. It builds on everything you've practiced so far. You'll use presence instead of fixing, comfort instead of distraction, and truth instead of platitudes. These are quiet skills, but they have a powerful long-term impact.

A short parent script that de-escalates without shaming might be, "That really hurts. I'm here with you." It doesn't solve the problem. It solves the loneliness.

Here's a gentle practice to begin this week. When sadness shows up, pause before responding. Count to three silently. Then choose a response that acknowledges the feeling rather than the solution. This small pause often changes the entire tone of the moment.

As always, if sadness becomes prolonged, intense, or begins to interfere significantly with daily life or safety, professional support can help both you and your child navigate what's going on. Support is part of care, not a sign of weakness.

8.1 Teaching Kids That Sadness Is Not a Problem to Fix

Many adults grew up learning that sadness should be minimized or hidden. "Don't cry." "Be strong." "Look on the bright side." These messages were often meant to protect, but they taught children to disconnect from an essential part of their emotional life. Teaching kids that sadness is not a problem to fix begins with unlearning our own urgency.

Validation is the cornerstone. Validation does not mean agreeing with the situation or amplifying despair. It means acknowledging the emotional reality without trying to change it. When a child is sad because a friend didn't invite them to a party, validation sounds like, "That really hurts." Not, "They probably forgot," or, "You didn't even want to go." The first response meets the feeling. The others step around it.

A vivid example with a preschooler shows this clearly. A three-year-old cries when their favorite cup breaks. The cup is replaceable. The feeling is not. When the parent kneels and says, "You loved that cup. It's okay to be sad," the child sobs for a minute, then leans in for a hug. When the parent says, "It's not a big deal," the crying often escalates. The difference is permission.

With older children, validation often feels harder because the problems feel bigger and the stakes feel higher. A ten-year-old who fails a test may spiral into self-criticism. The adult urge is to reassure quickly. "You're smart." "It's just one test." Validation asks you to slow down. "You're disappointed and embarrassed." That sentence doesn't trap the child in sadness. It opens the door for it to move.

Understanding the difference between comfort and distraction is crucial here. Comfort stays with the feeling. Distraction tries to replace it. Comfort sounds like sitting quietly together, offering a hug, or listening without interrupting. Distraction sounds like immediately suggesting a snack, a show, or a new activity. Distraction has its place, especially after the feeling has been acknowledged. When used too early, it can teach children that sadness is unacceptable.

Imagine a seven-year-old who loses a game and cries. A parent might say, "Do you want a hug or to sit together?" That's comfort. If the child cries for a bit and then naturally shifts, distraction might follow. "Want to go outside?" The order matters. Feel first. Move on later.

Normalizing tears and quiet is another important piece. Tears are a natural stress release. Quiet can be a form of processing. When adults label crying as weakness or silence as avoidance, children learn to perform emotions instead of feel them. You can normalize by naming what you see. "Your body is letting the sadness out." Or, "You're being quiet. I'll be nearby if you want company." These statements remove judgment and pressure.

A real-life example with an older child highlights this. A twelve-year-old experiences a friendship breakup and becomes withdrawn. The parent resists the urge to push conversation and instead says, "Breakups hurt. You don't have to talk right now." Over the next few days, the child slowly opens up. The space allowed the sadness to move instead of freeze.

A short parent script that supports this approach might be, "You don't have to be okay right now." Simple, steady, and deeply regulating.

There are common mistakes to avoid when supporting sadness. One is over-cheering, trying to replace sadness with positivity too quickly. Another is problem-solving immediately, which can make children feel like their feelings are inconvenient. A third is catastrophizing alongside the child, which can make sadness feel endless. These mistakes are human. Awareness allows for repair.

Here's a tiny practice to try today. When your child shows sadness, offer one sentence of validation and then stop talking. Sit with them for thirty seconds without fixing or distracting. Notice how your own body feels during that pause. This practice builds your capacity to tolerate sadness alongside your child.

Repair matters when sadness is mishandled. Imagine you brushed off your child's tears because you were rushed. Later, you can say, "Earlier I tried to hurry you out of being sad. I'm sorry. What you felt mattered." This repair teaches that emotions are always welcome, even when timing is imperfect.

Teaching kids that sadness is not a problem to fix doesn't mean leaving them alone in it indefinitely. It means trusting the natural arc of emotion. When sadness is met with presence, it often softens on its own. Children learn that they can feel deeply and still be okay.

As you move forward in this chapter, you'll explore how children build resilience around disappointment and how to support them through grief and big life changes. For now, stay with this foundation. Sadness doesn't need to be rushed. It needs to be witnessed. When children learn that, they carry a quiet strength into every part of their lives.

8.2 Disappointment Resilience

Disappointment is sadness with a future-facing edge. It's the feeling that arrives when hopes meet reality and don't match. Children experience disappointment constantly, often in small ways adults barely notice. The snack they wanted is gone. The park is closed. A friend chooses someone else to sit with. These moments are not failures of childhood. They are practice reps for living.

Helping children build disappointment resilience doesn't mean toughening them up or minimizing what they feel. It means teaching them how to bend without breaking. It means helping them grieve Plan A and slowly turn toward Plan B, even when they don't like it.

Plan A versus Plan B thinking is a powerful reframe for children of all ages. Plan A is what we hoped for. Plan B is what we do when Plan A doesn't happen. The key is teaching that having a Plan B doesn't mean Plan A didn't matter. It means life kept moving. When adults jump too quickly to Plan B, children often feel rushed through their sadness. When adults stay stuck in Plan A, children can feel helpless. The sweet spot is acknowledging the loss before pivoting.

A vivid example with a young child makes this clear. A five-year-old is promised a trip to the playground, but it starts raining. The child collapses into tears. Instead of immediately saying, "We'll play inside instead," the parent pauses and says, "You really wanted the playground. That's a big letdown." The child cries. After a moment, the parent adds, "That was Plan A. We need a Plan B for today." Together they choose a game inside. The disappointment doesn't disappear, but it softens enough to move forward.

With older children, Plan A losses can feel more personal. A ten-year-old doesn't get invited to a party they were excited about. The parent listens, validates, and resists the urge to explain or fix. Later, they might say, "It hurts when Plan A doesn't happen. When you're ready, we can think about Plan B, even if you still feel sad." This honors the emotion and builds flexibility.

Language matters here. Teaching children acceptance phrases gives them something to lean on when emotions spike. A phrase like, "I don't like it, but I can handle it," acknowledges discomfort without despair. It doesn't pretend the situation is okay. It affirms the child's capacity to cope. Younger children might shorten it to, "I don't like it, but I'm okay." Older children might add their own words. The goal is not perfection, but familiarity.

Building disappointment resilience also involves something called micro-recoveries. These are small, everyday disappointments used intentionally as practice. When a child chooses the broken cookie or waits an extra minute for a turn, and you stay present instead of rescuing, you're helping their nervous system learn recovery. Micro-recoveries are the emotional equivalent of small weights at the gym. They build strength gradually.

A real-life example shows this in action. A seven-year-old wants the blue cup, but it's in the dishwasher. The parent sees the disappointment rise and says, "You wanted blue. That's not available." They pause, breathe together, and add, "You can choose red or green." The child complains, then chooses. The world doesn't end. The child practices disappointment and recovery in a safe context.

A short parent script that de-escalates without shaming might be, "This isn't what you hoped for. You can be upset and still move forward." It names both realities.

Common mistakes can make disappointment harder. One is rushing to fix, which teaches children they can't tolerate discomfort. Another is dismissing disappointment as trivial, which can make children feel dramatic or unseen. A third is framing Plan B as a punishment, which adds resentment. These mistakes are understandable, especially when you're tired. Awareness creates room for change.

Here's a tiny practice to try today. When a small disappointment arises, resist the urge to immediately improve the situation. Name the disappointment once. Pause for ten seconds. Then offer a Plan B. Notice how your child responds when given space to feel first.

Repair matters when disappointment support goes off track. Imagine you brushed off a disappointment and your child shut down. Later, you can say, "Earlier, I moved past your disappointment too fast. I'm sorry. It mattered to you." This repair rebuilds trust and models emotional responsibility.

If disappointment frequently leads to intense distress or prolonged shutdown, professional support can help you explore what's underneath and build tailored strategies. Disappointment resilience grows best with steady support.

8.3 Grief and Big Life Changes

Grief is sadness stretched over time. It arrives with loss, change, and endings, even when those changes are not traditionally labeled as "loss." Children grieve moves, divorces, lost friendships, changing schools, and the death of people or pets. Grief in children is often misunderstood because it looks different from adult grief. It can come in waves, appear suddenly, and disappear just as quickly, only to return later.

One of the most important supports you can offer during grief is age-appropriate truth. Children sense when something is wrong. When adults use vague explanations to protect them, children often imagine something worse. Saying "They went away" or "Everything will be fine" can increase fear. Clear, simple truth builds safety, even when the truth is sad.

For a young child facing a move, age-appropriate truth might sound like, "We're moving to a new house. That means leaving this one. It's okay to feel sad about that." For a child grieving a pet, it might be, "Our dog's body stopped working. They died. We won't see them again." These words are hard to say, but they prevent confusion and anxiety.

Rituals help grief move. Children need concrete ways to process abstract loss. Rituals don't need to be elaborate. They need to be meaningful. A memory box where a child places drawings or photos. Writing letters to someone who moved away or passed on. Drawing pictures of what's missed. Creating a new routine to anchor the day. These acts give grief a container.

A vivid example illustrates this. A six-year-old loses a grandparent and becomes withdrawn. The parent creates a small ritual: every Sunday, they light a candle and share one memory. Sometimes the child talks. Sometimes they draw. The ritual becomes a predictable place for grief. Outside of it, the child returns to play. Grief has a home.

Supporting children through divorce or separation requires similar honesty and structure. Children need to know the change is not their fault and that both parents will continue to care for them. Repeating this message calmly over time matters more than saying it once. Grief here often shows up as regression, anger, or clinginess. These are not manipulations. They are attempts to regain safety.

Friendship breakups can be just as painful as family losses, especially for older children. An eleven-year-old who loses a close friend may feel rejected and ashamed. Minimizing this loss can deepen the hurt. Validating it sounds like, "Losing a friend hurts a lot. I'm really sorry." From there, you can offer support without rushing replacement friendships.

A short parent script that supports grief without shaming might be, "Something important changed, and it makes sense to feel sad about it." This normalizes the response and removes pressure to "be okay."

Common mistakes in supporting grief include avoiding the topic entirely, which can make children feel alone, or repeatedly checking in with heavy questions, which can feel intrusive. Another mistake is expecting grief to follow a timeline. Children may seem fine for weeks and then fall apart unexpectedly. This is normal.

Here's a tiny practice to try today. Ask your child one open-ended question about a past change, like a move or lost friendship. "What do you miss most?" Listen without correcting or fixing. Thank them for sharing. This keeps the door open.

Repair after grief missteps matters deeply. Imagine you tried to cheer your child up when they were grieving and they withdrew. Later, you might say, "I tried to make you feel better when you were sad. I see now you needed me to listen. I'm sorry." This repair restores emotional safety.

If grief seems to overwhelm your child for long periods, interferes with daily functioning, or is paired with concerning behaviors, professional support can help your family navigate the process. Grief deserves care and companionship.

Sadness, disappointment, and grief are not detours from healthy development. They are part of it. When you help your child let these feelings move through with honesty, ritual, and support, you're teaching them one of the most enduring skills of all: how to live fully, even when life hurts.

Chapter 9 Emotional Coaching at Home: Daily Habits That Change Everything

You don't need perfect parenting. You need predictable emotional habits that repeat. That's the quiet truth most families discover over time. Change rarely comes from one big conversation or a perfectly handled meltdown. It comes from small, steady moments that add up. Emotional coaching at home is not about adding another item to your to-do list. It's about shaping the moments you already have so they teach skills instead of just getting through the day.

If you've been following week by week, you've already built a strong foundation. You've learned to read behavior as communication, to notice body signals, to co-regulate, to hold boundaries without threats, and to support big feelings like anger, anxiety, and sadness. This chapter brings all of that into daily life. It's about turning theory into rhythm.

Many parents imagine emotional coaching as something formal or time-consuming. In reality, it works best when it's brief, predictable, and woven into routines. Children don't need deep processing every day. They need repetition. They need to know there's a reliable place where emotions are noticed, named, and handled with care.

Think of emotional coaching like brushing teeth. You don't wait for a cavity to start brushing. You do it regularly, even when things seem fine. The same is true here. When emotional skills are practiced during calm moments, they're more likely to show up when things are hard.

A vivid example comes from a busy family with two working parents and three kids. Evenings are chaotic. Homework, dinner, baths, bedtime. Emotional conversations often get skipped because everyone is tired. When the parents introduce a simple daily emotional routine, just a few minutes at the same time each evening, something shifts. The kids begin bringing up small worries and frustrations before they explode. The household doesn't become magically calm, but it becomes more connected and less reactive.

Another example looks quieter. A single parent with a sensitive six-year-old notices that afternoons often end in tears. Instead of addressing each meltdown as it comes, the parent adds a short check-in during the car ride home. Over time, the child starts naming feelings earlier. The meltdowns don't disappear, but they shorten. The child feels less alone with their emotions.

Emotional coaching is not about fixing children. It's about walking alongside them as they learn how emotions work. It's about showing, through repetition, that feelings are welcome and manageable. When this becomes part of the culture at home, children stop testing whether emotions are safe. They know.

A short parent script that de-escalates without shaming might be, "We can talk about feelings for a minute. You're not in trouble." That sentence alone can lower defenses and invite honesty.

Here's a gentle practice to start this week. Choose one consistent time of day when you're usually with your child, even briefly. It might be after school, during dinner, or at bedtime. Commit to using that time for emotional coaching most days, even if it's just two or three minutes. Consistency matters more than length.

As always, if emotional struggles feel overwhelming or safety becomes a concern, professional support can help you tailor these habits to your family's needs. Daily coaching works best when it's part of a wider support system, not a replacement for help when help is needed.

9.1 The 5-Minute Daily Emotional Routine

The heart of emotional coaching at home is a short, repeatable routine. Five minutes is enough. Less than five can work too. What matters is that your child knows when and how emotions will be invited into the conversation. Predictability creates safety.

The routine begins with a check-in that doesn't feel intrusive. Many children shut down when asked, "How did you feel today?" It's too big, too direct, or too loaded. Instead, gentle prompts work better. You might ask, "Was there a part of today that felt hard?" or "Did anything make your body feel big today?" For younger children, you can offer choices. "Was today more fun or more frustrating?" These questions give children an entry point without pressure.

A real-life example with a preschooler shows this well. A four-year-old is asked at dinner, "What was the hardest part of your day?" They think for a moment and say, "Cleanup." The parent nods and says, "Cleanup felt hard." That's it. No lecture. No fixing. The child feels heard.

With an older child, the check-in can be more reflective. A ten-year-old might be asked, "What's one thing that stuck with you today?" The child shrugs, then says, "Math." The parent waits and gently adds, "Was math more confusing or more stressful?" The conversation unfolds naturally.

The second part of the routine is reflect and label. This is where you mirror what you hear and offer emotional language. "Sounds like you felt left out." "That was disappointing." "You were nervous and excited at the same time." You're not correcting the child's experience. You're helping them organize it. This step builds emotional vocabulary and self-awareness.

A vivid example with a school-age child illustrates the power of reflection. An eight-year-old complains angrily about a friend. The parent reflects, "It sounds like you felt hurt and then angry." The child pauses and says, "Yeah. Mostly hurt." That shift matters. Naming the softer feeling underneath often changes the tone of the conversation.

The routine ends with one simple skill practice. This is not a long lesson. It's a quick, embodied action that reinforces coping. You might take one slow breath together. You might shake out your arms and legs for ten seconds. You might practice a choice script like, "I don't like it, but I can handle it." The skill practice anchors the conversation in the body, where emotions actually live.

For a young child, the skill might be blowing out an imaginary candle. For an older child, it might be placing a hand on the chest and noticing the breath. The point is not to calm everything down perfectly. It's to practice having a tool.

A short parent script that keeps this routine light could be, "Let's do our quick feelings check." Familiar words reduce resistance over time.

Common mistakes can derail the routine. One is turning it into an interrogation, asking too many follow-up questions. Another is skipping reflection and jumping straight to advice. A third is using the routine only when something went wrong, which can make it feel like a disciplinary tool. Keeping it brief and neutral helps it stay safe.

Here's a tiny practice to try today. Choose one check-in question and one skill practice. Write them down or say them out loud to yourself. Use the same ones for a week. Notice how repetition changes your child's comfort level.

Repair is part of emotional coaching too. Imagine you rushed through the routine one evening and your child snapped, "Never mind." Later, you can say, "I was distracted earlier and didn't really listen. I'm sorry. Tomorrow we can try again." This models accountability and shows that emotional space is flexible, not fragile.

Another repair example might follow a moment when you mislabel a feeling. If you said, "You were angry," and your child said, "No, I was scared," you can respond later with, "Thanks for correcting me. I'm still learning your feelings." This reinforces trust and agency.

Over time, this five-minute routine becomes a container. Children begin to save thoughts for it. Parents begin to notice patterns sooner. Emotions become part of daily life, not emergencies. That's when real change happens.

Emotional coaching doesn't require special training or endless patience. It requires presence, repetition, and humility. Some days the routine will feel smooth. Other days it will feel awkward or rushed. Both are okay. The power is in showing up again and again.

As you move forward, remember that you're not teaching children to control their emotions. You're teaching them to understand and use them. These small, daily habits build a lifelong skill set. Five minutes at a time, you're changing how emotions live in your home.

9.2 Emotion Coaching Language That Builds Trust

Language is one of the most powerful tools you use as a parent, often without realizing it. The words you choose in emotional moments don't just communicate information. They communicate safety. Over time, children learn whether emotions are welcome, tolerated, or pushed aside based largely on how adults talk to them when feelings are big.

Emotion coaching language builds trust when it opens connection instead of closing it. Opening language sounds curious, reflective, and steady. It leaves room for the child's experience to exist. Closing language sounds dismissive, rushed, or overly corrective, even when it's meant to help. The difference is often subtle, but the impact is lasting.

Consider a moment with a seven-year-old who comes home upset after school and snaps, "I hate school." A closing response might be, "You don't hate school. You like school." The adult is trying to correct an exaggeration, but the child hears, "You're wrong about your feelings." An opening response sounds different. "Something at school made today really hard." That response doesn't agree with the statement, but it honors the feeling underneath it.

Phrases that open connection often begin with reflection. "Sounds like you felt left out." "That was really frustrating." "You were excited and then disappointed." These phrases don't fix the problem. They organize the experience. When children feel understood, their nervous systems settle enough to think and talk.

Closing phrases often sneak in unintentionally. "You're okay" said too soon can shut down expression. "It's not a big deal" can make children feel silly or dramatic. "You'll be fine" can feel dismissive when fear is real. None of these phrases are harmful in isolation. The issue is timing. When they come before a child feels heard, they can break trust.

A vivid example shows how this plays out with a younger child. A four-year-old cries because their block tower falls. An adult says, "You're okay, just build it again." The child cries harder. The adult then tries, "That was disappointing. You worked hard on it." The child's shoulders drop. Tears slow. Same situation, different language, different outcome.

With older children, language becomes even more important because they are more sensitive to perceived judgment. A ten-year-old might say, "I'm so stupid," after making a mistake. A closing response would be, "Don't say that." An opening response might be, "It sounds like you're really frustrated with yourself." From there, you can gently challenge the self-talk once the emotion is acknowledged.

Emotion coaching language also includes what you say when you've made a mistake. Apologizing as a parent is one of the most trust-building acts you can model. It shows children that power and accountability can coexist. An apology doesn't undermine authority. It strengthens it.

A genuine apology is simple and specific. "I raised my voice earlier when you were upset. I'm sorry." You don't add excuses. You don't demand forgiveness. You don't flip it back onto the child. You model responsibility. This teaches children that relationships can stretch and repair, even when emotions get messy.

A real-life example with a school-age child illustrates this well. A parent snaps during homework time and later feels regret. At bedtime, the parent says, "Earlier I was impatient when you were struggling. I'm sorry. You didn't deserve that." The child nods and says, "It made me feel bad." The parent listens and replies, "Thank you for telling me." Trust deepens.

A short parent script that de-escalates without shaming might be, "I want to understand, not fix you." That sentence alone can shift the tone of a conversation.

Common mistakes with emotion coaching language often come from good intentions. One mistake is over-teaching in the moment, turning every feeling into a lesson. Another is using reflective language mechanically, which can sound insincere. A third is apologizing in a way that shifts responsibility, such as saying, "I'm sorry you made me yell." These patterns can erode trust over time. Awareness allows for change.

Here's a tiny practice to try today. Choose one reflective phrase, such as "That sounds really hard," and use it the next time your child shows emotion. Say it once and then pause. Notice how the pause changes the interaction.

Repair after a hard moment with language is powerful. Imagine you dismissed your child's feelings earlier. Later, you might say, "I told you it wasn't a big deal, and I see now that it was to you. I'm sorry. Do you want to tell me more?" This repair teaches that emotional safety can be restored, even after missteps.

Emotion coaching language isn't about saying the perfect thing. It's about staying aligned with your child's experience more often than not. Over time, children internalize this language. They learn how to talk to themselves with the same respect and clarity you offer them.

9.3 Turning Everyday Moments Into Lessons

One of the biggest myths about emotional learning is that it requires special time, special tools, or serious conversations. In reality, the best teaching moments are already built into your day. They happen when pressure is low and connection is natural. Car rides, meals, and bedtime are especially rich windows for emotional coaching.

Car rides work well because there's no need for eye contact. Many children open up more when they don't feel watched. A casual question like, "What was the best and hardest part of today?" can invite sharing without intensity. Silence is okay too. Sometimes emotional processing happens simply because the space is available.

Mealtimes offer a chance to normalize emotions as part of family life. When adults share age-appropriate feelings from their own day, children learn that emotions are not just a "kid thing." A parent might say, "I felt frustrated at work today, and I took a walk to calm down." This models regulation without burdening the child.

Bedtime is another powerful moment because the nervous system is slowing down. Gentle reflection fits naturally here. A parent might say, "Was there anything that felt heavy today?" or "Is there anything you want help carrying into tomorrow?" These questions don't demand answers. They offer availability.

Games make emotional learning playful and accessible. Emotion charades can involve acting out feelings with faces and bodies, then guessing together. This builds emotional literacy without pressure. A game like "high/low" invites sharing one good thing and one hard thing from the day. "What would you tell a friend?" helps children practice compassion and problem-solving by shifting perspective.

A vivid example shows how this works with siblings. During dinner, a parent suggests "high/low." One child shares a high. The other shrugs. The parent shares their own low. The second child then shares too. The routine becomes familiar. Over time, children anticipate it and bring more depth.

With older children, everyday moments can include hypothetical questions. During a walk, a parent might ask, "If your friend was worried about tomorrow, what would you tell them?" The child answers thoughtfully. The parent listens. This builds empathy and cognitive flexibility without lecturing.

Celebrating effort rather than emotional "perfection" is key. Children don't need praise for being calm all the time. They need acknowledgment for trying. "You were really angry, and you used your words." "You felt nervous and still walked into class." These statements reinforce courage and skill use, not suppression.

A short parent script that supports this mindset might be, "You're learning how to handle big feelings, and I see the effort." It focuses on growth, not outcomes.

Common mistakes when turning everyday moments into lessons include overloading children with questions, which can feel intrusive, or turning games into evaluations. Another mistake is only pointing out emotional growth when things go well, instead of also acknowledging effort during hard moments. Keeping things light and relational helps these moments stay effective.

Here's a tiny practice to try today. Choose one routine you already do, such as brushing teeth or driving to school. Add one gentle emotional question to that routine for the next few days. Keep it the same question. Notice how repetition changes comfort.

Repair is part of this process too. Imagine you tried to turn a moment into a lesson and your child rolled their eyes or shut down. Later, you can say, "I think I pushed a conversation when you weren't in the mood. I'm sorry. We can talk another time." This models respect for boundaries and emotional timing.

Turning everyday moments into lessons doesn't mean every moment becomes a teaching opportunity. It means you're available when opportunities naturally arise. Some days will be rich with conversation. Other days will be quiet. Both are okay.

When emotional coaching is woven into daily life, children don't feel like they're being analyzed or managed. They feel accompanied. Over time, they begin to use the language, games, and reflections on their own. They ask better questions. They recover faster. They trust that emotions belong in relationships.

If everyday moments consistently feel charged or disconnected despite your efforts, outside support can help you reset patterns and find new entry points. Support can refresh your approach and ease the load.

Emotional coaching at home isn't about doing more. It's about doing what you already do with a little more intention. Small habits, repeated daily, change everything.

Chapter 10 Thriving Long-Term: Confidence, Empathy, and Emotional Strength

Emotional strength isn't toughness. It's flexibility. It's the ability to feel deeply, recover steadily, and connect honestly. By the time families reach this chapter, many of the loud fires have already been addressed. You've learned how to respond to meltdowns without shame, how to guide anger safely, how to support anxiety and sadness, and how to coach emotions in everyday life. This chapter zooms out. It asks a longer-term question: what does all this work grow into?

Thriving emotionally does not mean children stop struggling. It means they develop a growing trust in themselves and in relationships. They learn that discomfort is information, not danger. They learn that mistakes can be repaired. They learn that who they are matters more than how they perform. These lessons don't arrive all at once. They arrive slowly, through repetition, modeling, and thousands of small moments that tell a child, "You can handle life, and you don't have to do it alone."

A vivid example comes from a nine-year-old who once melted down daily after school. Over time, with consistent emotional coaching, those meltdowns shortened. Then they changed shape. Instead of screaming, the child began saying, "I need a break." Eventually, the child began planning ahead, asking for a snack or quiet time. The emotions didn't disappear. The child's relationship with them changed. That is emotional strength in action.

Another example looks quieter. A five-year-old who once clung at drop-off now still feels nervous, but walks into class with a wave. The fear hasn't vanished. The child has learned, through experience and support, "I can feel this and still go." That belief will show up again and again throughout life.

Long-term thriving also depends on what children absorb about themselves. Are they only praised for outcomes, or are they seen for their inner signals and efforts? Do they learn to override hunger, exhaustion, or discomfort to please others, or do they learn to listen inwardly? Do they experience empathy as a skill that includes boundaries, or as pressure to keep others comfortable at their own expense? These questions shape confidence and connection far more than any single strategy.

A short parent script that supports long-term thriving without shaming might be, "You're learning how to listen to yourself. I trust that process." This communicates confidence in the child's internal growth, not just their behavior.

Here's a simple practice to hold alongside this chapter. Once this week, notice a moment when your child listens to an internal signal, even a small one. They stop eating when full. They ask for space. They say no. Name it neutrally. "You noticed what your body needed." This builds self-trust without pressure.

As always, if at any point emotional struggles intensify, feel confusing, or raise concerns about safety or daily functioning, professional support can be an important and caring step. Thriving long-term includes knowing when to widen the circle of support.

10.1 Raising Self-Trust and Inner Confidence

Confidence is often misunderstood as boldness or ease. In reality, inner confidence grows from self-trust. Self-trust is the belief that your signals matter and that you can respond to them wisely. Children who trust themselves are not fearless. They are grounded. They know how to listen inwardly and outwardly at the same time.

Teaching kids to trust their signals begins early and continues throughout childhood. Signals include hunger, fatigue, excitement, discomfort, curiosity, and intuition. When adults consistently override these signals, often unintentionally, children learn to doubt themselves. When adults notice and respect signals, children learn that their inner world is reliable.

A common moment illustrates this clearly. A three-year-old says they're hungry shortly after a meal. An adult might respond, "You just ate, you can't be hungry." Sometimes that's true. Sometimes it's not. A signal-respecting response sounds different. "Your body says it's hungry. Let's check if it needs a snack or water." The child learns that signals can be explored, not dismissed.

With older children, signals become more complex. A ten-year-old might say they don't want to go to a sleepover. Adults may worry about avoidance and push. Sometimes encouragement is helpful. Other times, the child is picking up on discomfort they can't yet name. Supporting self-trust sounds like, "You're unsure. Let's talk about what your body is telling you." The decision might still be to go, but the process includes listening instead of overriding.

Encouraging autonomy through structured choices is another powerful way to build confidence. Autonomy doesn't mean unlimited freedom. It means having a say within clear boundaries. Structured choices give children practice making decisions and living with outcomes. "Do you want to start homework before or after your snack?" "Do you want the red shirt or the blue one?" These choices are small, but they reinforce a sense of agency.

A vivid example with a preschooler shows how this works. A four-year-old resists getting dressed. Instead of forcing compliance, the parent offers two weather-appropriate outfits. The child chooses one. The struggle dissolves. More importantly, the child experiences themselves as capable. Over time, these moments accumulate into confidence.

With school-age children, autonomy can expand. A nine-year-old might choose the order of their chores or how to break a task into steps. The adult still holds the boundary that the task gets done, but the child practices decision-making within it. This balance teaches responsibility without control.

Helping kids build identity beyond achievement is perhaps one of the most important long-term protections you can offer. Many children quickly learn that praise follows performance. Good grades, goals scored, behavior praised publicly. When identity becomes tied to outcomes, confidence becomes fragile. A setback feels like a verdict on who they are.

Shifting this pattern doesn't require eliminating praise. It requires broadening it. Notice qualities, not just results. Curiosity, persistence, honesty, creativity, kindness toward self. When a child fails a test, you might say, "I saw how hard you studied," or "I noticed you asked for help when it got confusing." These statements reinforce identity as something deeper than success.

A real-life example with an older child illustrates this shift. An eleven-year-old who excels academically melts down after a poor grade. The parent resists reassuring with "You're smart." Instead, they say, "This hurts because you care. Being a learner means sometimes things don't go as planned." The child gradually learns that mistakes don't erase worth.

Language around boundaries also plays a role in self-trust. When children say no and adults listen, within reason, children learn that boundaries are allowed. When children express discomfort and adults investigate instead of dismiss, children learn that intuition matters. This doesn't mean every boundary can be honored. It means every boundary can be respected as information.

A short parent script that supports this might be, "Let's listen to what your body is saying and decide together." It invites collaboration without giving up leadership.

Common mistakes can undermine self-trust even with the best intentions. One is over-praising outcomes, which can create pressure. Another is rescuing too quickly, which sends the message that the child can't handle discomfort. A third is dismissing signals because they're inconvenient. These patterns are understandable. Awareness allows you to recalibrate.

Here's a tiny practice to try today. The next time your child expresses a preference or discomfort, reflect it before responding. "You're feeling done," or "You're unsure." Pause. Then decide together what to do next. This pause teaches that signals are part of decision-making.

Repair is essential when self-trust gets shaken. Imagine you pushed your child to do something and later realized you missed an important signal. You can say, "I didn't listen carefully earlier. I'm sorry. Your signals matter to me." This repair doesn't undo the moment, but it rebuilds trust.

If a child consistently ignores their own needs, shows extreme people-pleasing, or struggles to identify internal signals, additional support can help strengthen these skills. Self-trust grows best with guidance and patience.

Raising self-trust and inner confidence is not about creating certainty. It's about creating a steady inner reference point. When children learn to listen to themselves, make choices, and see their worth beyond achievement, they carry something powerful into adulthood. They carry a sense of self that can bend, recover, and keep growing, even when life gets hard.

10.2 Teaching Empathy Without People-Pleasing

Empathy is often praised as one of the most important traits we can raise in children. We want kids who notice others, care about impact, and act with kindness. But empathy without boundaries can quietly turn into people-pleasing. When children learn that being "nice" means ignoring their own needs, saying yes when they want to say no, or taking responsibility for other people's feelings, empathy stops being a strength and starts becoming a burden.

Teaching empathy well means teaching it alongside self-respect. It means helping children understand others without disappearing themselves. This balance doesn't come naturally. It's learned through modeling, language, and repeated experiences where kindness and boundaries coexist.

Perspective-taking is the foundation of empathy. It's the ability to imagine what someone else might be feeling without assuming or mind-reading. With young children, this begins very simply. When a toddler grabs a toy and another child cries, an adult might say, "Your friend is crying. That looks upsetting for them." The goal isn't to shame the child into compliance. It's to draw attention to impact in a neutral way.

As children grow, perspective-taking can become more nuanced. A seven-year-old might complain, "He's so annoying." A parent can respond, "You're really frustrated. I wonder what it felt like for him when that happened." The word wonder matters. It invites curiosity instead of accusation. Curiosity keeps empathy from turning into blame.

Compassionate action is the next step. This is where children learn how to respond once they notice someone else's feelings. Compassionate action does not always mean fixing or agreeing.

Sometimes it means offering help. Sometimes it means giving space. Sometimes it means saying sorry. Children need guidance here, because many assume compassion means self-sacrifice.

A vivid example illustrates this. A five-year-old notices a classmate crying because they lost a game. The child wants to give up their own prize to make the other child feel better. The instinct is generous, but the adult pauses and says, "You can care about your friend and still keep your prize. You could say, 'I'm sorry you're sad.'" The child learns that compassion doesn't require giving up something important to them.

With older children, people-pleasing often shows up in friendships. A ten-year-old might feel pressured to agree with friends to avoid conflict. When they come home exhausted and irritable, the parent listens and reflects, "It sounds like you were trying really hard to keep everyone happy." Then the parent adds, "Being kind doesn't mean saying yes when it doesn't feel right." This sentence can be life-changing when repeated over time.

Teaching respectful curiosity helps children ask instead of assume. Instead of "Why are you so mad?" they can learn to say, "Are you okay?" Instead of guessing intentions, they can ask clarifying questions. This skill protects children from both conflict and self-blame.

Boundaries are where empathy gets tested. Children need explicit permission to have limits, especially when they care deeply. Saying no can feel unkind to a child who has been praised for being helpful or agreeable. Adults can normalize this by modeling boundary language themselves. "I want to help, and I'm not able to right now." "I care about you, and I need a break." When children hear these phrases regularly, they internalize the message that kindness includes honesty.

A real-life example with a school-age child shows this balance. An eight-year-old agrees to play a game they hate because their friend insists. Later, the child melts down at home. The parent reflects, "You tried to be kind, and it cost you." Then they add, "Next time, you could say, 'I don't want to play that. Let's choose something else.' That's still kind." The child practices the sentence out loud. Empathy and boundaries become partners instead of rivals.

Repair after hurting others is another essential empathy skill. Children will hurt people. This is not a failure. It's part of learning. What matters is how repair is handled. Repair that focuses only on consequences can create shame. Repair that combines accountability and compassion teaches responsibility.

A healthy repair sounds like, "What happened?" followed by, "Who was affected?" and then, "What can help now?" The adult stays calm and supportive, guiding the child to take responsibility without labeling them as bad. A child who hit in anger might say sorry, help get ice, or write a note later. The action matters less than the understanding.

A short parent script that de-escalates without shaming might be, "You care about others, and your needs matter too." This sentence holds both sides of empathy at once.

Common mistakes can quietly undermine this work. One is praising children only for being nice or helpful, which can teach them to suppress discomfort. Another is framing empathy as obligation, such as forcing apologies before understanding. A third is rescuing children from all relational discomfort, which prevents them from practicing boundaries. These patterns are common and correctable.

Here's a tiny practice to try today. The next time your child shows empathy, name both sides. "You noticed how they felt, and you spoke up for yourself." This reinforces balance.

Repair matters here too. Imagine you pressured your child to share or apologize when they weren't ready. Later, you can say, "I pushed you to be kind without listening to how you felt. I'm sorry. Both matter." This repair models exactly the empathy-with-boundaries you're trying to teach.

If a child consistently ignores their own needs, feels responsible for others' emotions, or shows intense distress around conflict, professional support can help untangle people-pleasing patterns early. Early guidance protects long-term well-being.

10.3 A Family Emotional Plan (So Skills Stick)

Skills stick when they're supported by environment, not just intention. Families who thrive emotionally don't rely on memory or willpower alone. They create simple structures that make regulation, repair, and connection easier during real life.

A family emotional plan doesn't need to be formal or written down, though it can be. It's an agreement, often unspoken at first, about how emotions are handled in your home. This plan brings together everything you've practiced throughout this book and makes it sustainable.

One practical element of this plan is creating a home regulation toolbox space. This is a physical place where calming and coping tools live. It might be a basket, a drawer, or a corner. What matters is accessibility and familiarity. The toolbox might include soft items, drawing materials, movement prompts, or sensory supports that work for your family. The tools are introduced during calm times and used during hard ones without fanfare.

A vivid example shows this in action. A family with a highly sensitive six-year-old sets up a small shelf in the living room. It holds paper, crayons, a stress ball, and a soft blanket. When emotions rise, the parent says, "The toolbox is there if you want it." Over time, the child begins to go there independently. Regulation becomes something the child does, not something done to them.

Family agreements are another key piece. These are not rules posted on the wall. They are shared understandings revisited over time. Agreements might include how anger is expressed, how conflicts are handled, how mistakes are repaired, and how apologies work. The tone is collaborative, not authoritarian.

For example, a family might agree that anger is allowed, but hurting is not. They might agree that yelling means someone needs help calming down, not punishment. They might agree that apologies include listening and making amends, not just saying words. These agreements are modeled by adults first. Children learn them through experience.

A real-life example with siblings illustrates this. Two siblings argue loudly. Instead of sending them to separate rooms, the parent says, "Remember our agreement. We slow down and use words." The parent stays nearby to support. Later, the siblings talk it through and repair. The agreement gives structure without threats.

Knowing when to seek extra support is also part of a healthy emotional plan. Emotional coaching is powerful, but it's not meant to replace professional help when challenges exceed what a family can safely handle alone. Signs that extra support may be useful include emotions that consistently interfere with daily life, intense behaviors that don't improve with support, or safety concerns. Seeking help is not a failure of the plan. It's part of it.

A short parent script that supports this mindset might be, "We all need help sometimes. That's part of taking care of ourselves." This normalizes support instead of framing it as last resort.

Common mistakes with family emotional plans include making them too complicated, expecting children to remember them perfectly under stress, or using them as leverage during conflict. Another mistake is setting agreements but not modeling them as adults. Children learn far more from what you do than what you declare.

Here's a tiny practice to try today. Choose one family agreement to name out loud, such as how you handle mistakes. Say it calmly during a neutral moment. Repeat it the next time it's relevant. Repetition builds culture.

Repair after a breakdown in the plan is essential. Imagine you reacted harshly during a conflict, contradicting your family agreements. Later, you can say, "I didn't follow our agreement earlier. I'm sorry. I'm working on it too." This repair strengthens the plan instead of weakening it.

Over time, a family emotional plan becomes invisible. It shows up in tone, pacing, and expectations. Children grow up knowing what happens when emotions run high. They know repair is possible. They know they won't be shamed for feeling, and they won't be left alone with it either.

Thriving long-term doesn't come from getting everything right. It comes from creating a family environment where emotions are expected, skills are practiced, and connection is repaired again and again. When children grow up in that environment, they

don't just cope. They carry emotional strength forward, quietly
and confidently, into every relationship they build.

Conclusion — Your Child Doesn't Need Perfect Calm, They Need Safe Support

If there is one idea to carry with you as you close this book, let it be this: progress in emotional growth rarely looks like constant calm. It looks like fewer intense episodes, faster recoveries, and better repair when things go sideways. It looks like a child who still feels deeply, but no longer feels alone inside those feelings. It looks like a parent who doesn't panic at emotion, even when they're tired, even when they make mistakes.

Many parents begin this journey hoping to "fix" meltdowns, anxiety, anger, or sadness. Along the way, something more durable often emerges. You start noticing patterns instead of just behaviors. You start responding instead of reacting. You begin trusting that emotions are not emergencies, even when they're loud. This shift doesn't erase hard moments, but it changes how those moments live in your family.

Reframing progress is essential here. If you're measuring success by how rarely your child cries, yells, worries, or shuts down, you'll feel discouraged quickly. Emotional health is not the absence of emotion. A more accurate measure is intensity, duration, and repair. Are big feelings a little less explosive than they used to be? Do they pass a little more quickly? When things go badly, do you and your child find your way back to each other more often? Those are signs of growth.

You may notice that your child still has meltdowns, but now they can say, "I need help," sooner. You may see anxiety still show up, but your child is willing to take small brave steps instead of freezing completely. You may hear anger expressed with words instead of hands more often than before. These changes are easy to overlook because they're subtle. They are also profound.

The lifelong gift you are building is not compliance or emotional polish. It is capacity. Children who grow up with emotional coaching learn how to name what they feel, regulate their bodies, and stay connected to others even when emotions run high. They learn that feelings carry information, not shame. They learn that mistakes can be repaired. They learn that support is available, and that they are also capable.

This gift reaches far beyond childhood. It shows up in friendships where conflict can be navigated instead of avoided. It shows up in adolescence when identity feels shaky and emotions run hot. It shows up in adulthood as self-trust, empathy with boundaries, and resilience in the face of loss or change. You are not just helping your child get through today. You are shaping how they will meet the world.

As you think about next steps, simplicity matters more than ambition. You do not need to use every strategy from this book at once. In fact, trying to do too much often leads to burnout and inconsistency. A steadier approach is to choose a small set of tools and practice them until they feel familiar.

Here is a grounded 14-day starter plan to help you integrate what you've learned without overwhelm. For the next two weeks, choose three tools that resonated most with you. Perhaps it's the five-minute daily emotional check-in, a specific co-regulation script, and one body-based calming strategy. Or maybe it's Plan A versus Plan B language, a safe anger outlet, and a consistent bedtime wind-down. Pick tools that fit your family's real life, not an idealized version of it.

For fourteen days, focus only on those three tools. Use them imperfectly. Some days you'll remember. Some days you won't. That's okay. The goal is exposure, not mastery. You're building muscle memory, both for yourself and for your child. Around day five or six, you may notice resistance. That's normal too. New patterns can feel strange before they feel helpful.

During this two-week period, track progress lightly, without perfectionism. You don't need a chart or a scorecard unless that genuinely helps you. Instead, notice trends. Are you recovering more quickly after hard moments? Are you catching yourself before escalating more often? Is your child naming feelings a little sooner, even if the feelings are still big? These observations matter more than counting successes.

You might try a brief reflection every few days. Ask yourself, "What felt slightly easier this week?" or "Where did connection return faster than it used to?" Write a sentence or two if that helps, or simply note it mentally. Progress in emotional work is often quiet. You have to look gently to see it.

After fourteen days, add one new skill if it feels supportive. Not because you should, but because your foundation is stronger. Skills stack best when the ground beneath them is steady. If life feels particularly intense, it's also okay to pause and keep practicing what you've already chosen. There is no deadline on emotional growth.

Along the way, you will make mistakes. You will snap, rush, minimize, or forget everything you've read here in moments of stress. This does not undo your work. In fact, how you handle those moments may be the most important teaching of all. When you repair, you show your child that relationships can bend without breaking. When you apologize, you model accountability without shame. When you try again, you teach resilience in action.

Tracking progress without perfectionism also means noticing your own growth. Are you more curious than you used to be when emotions show up? Are you less afraid of your child's sadness or anger? Do you trust yourself to handle hard moments more than before? These internal shifts are just as important as changes you see in your child.

A final reassurance matters here, especially for parents who worry they should be able to handle everything on their own. Seeking help when you need it is not a failure of emotional coaching. It is part of it. There are times when emotions are intense, patterns feel stuck, or safety becomes a concern. In those moments, professional support can offer perspective, tools, and relief. It can widen the circle of care around your family.

Asking for help also teaches your child something vital. It teaches that support is a strength, not a weakness. It teaches that big feelings deserve attention and care. It teaches that no one is meant to carry everything alone.

As you close this book, remember that connection is the foundation. Skills grow best in safety. Techniques matter, but relationship matters more. Your presence, your willingness to listen, your commitment to repair, and your belief in your child's capacity are what make the skills stick.

Your child doesn't need you to be perfectly calm. They need you to be safe enough, steady enough, and willing enough to walk with them through the full range of human emotion. When you do that, again and again, you are giving them something enduring. You are teaching them that feelings are not obstacles to life. They are part of it. And they can be met with courage, compassion, and connection.